Bert Harned M.D.
Kerry L. Skinner, Editor

Any Ole Bush
Copyright © 2008 by Bert Harned
Published by
KLS LifeChange Ministries, Mobile, AL 36693

Dewey Decimal Classification: 248.4
Subject Heading: Christian Life

Library of Congress Cataloging-in-Publication Data

Harned, Bert, 1924–
Skinner, Kerry L., 1955–
    Any Ole Bush/Bert Harned, 1st edition
    p. cm.
    Includes bibliographic references.

    ISBN–0-9648743-7-7
    ISBN–13: 978-0-9648743-7-4

1. Christian life–Discipleship 2. Holy Spirit. I. Title.

All rights reserved. Printed in the United States of America. No part of this book may be used or reproduced in any manner whatsoever without written permission except in the case of brief quotations embodied in critical articles and reviews.

For more information contact:
Bert Harned, 1912 E. Catamaran Circle, Gilbert, AZ 85234 or
www.bertsgoodstuff.com

All scripture quotations, unless otherwise indicated, are taken from the HOLY BIBLE, NEW INTERNATIONAL VERSION®. NIV®. Copyright © 1973, 1978, 1984 by International Bible Society. Used by permission of Zondervan. All rights reserved.

Verses marked Phillips are taken from J.B. Phillips: The New Testament in Modern English. (D 1958, 1960.) Used by permission of Macmillan Publishing Company.

Scripture quotations marked (AMP) are taken from the Amplified Bible, Copyright © 1954, 1958, 1962, 1964, 1965, 1987 by The Lockman Foundation. Used by permission.

Contents

About the Author 5
Foreword..7
Preface 11
Acknowledgements..13
   1. The Big Picture...15
   2. A Disciple–A Bush on Fire..25
   3. The 1-ON-1: Our Game Plan 35
   4. The Holy Spirit–The Fire in the Bush 51
   5. Spirit-Controlled Helps 63
   6. Obedience–How Much is Enough? 71
   7. Life Purpose 89
   8. Potholes on the Road to Discipleship 95
   9. Valuable Suggestions 105
   Appendix..119

Dr. Bert Harned has spent a half century impacting countless lives (mine being one) with his discipleship methods. I am incredibly grateful for him and this book and you will be too.

Russ Crosson, CEO of Ron Blue & Co.

Bert Harned has been the voice of wisdom and truth in my life for most of the past 20 years. I am just one of the many, many men who could and have said this for 5 or 6 decades. During that period of time Bert's life has been a wonderful journey–(as our friend Mr. Buford would say)–from Success to Significance.

Ron Rossello
Business Owner
Elder at Grace Community Church in Tempe, Arizona

For over 40 years, Dr. Bert Harned has been discipling men and women as to what it means to walk in the Spirit. The extent of his quiet, yet profound influence in the lives of hundreds of believers is impossible to know, but is undoubtedly enormous. In his book, "Any Ole Bush," Bert dispenses a wealth of instruction that will assist any believer in experiencing greater intimacy with Christ. I know you will derive great benefit from the wisdom it contains.

Kevin Seacat
Seacat Financial Services
Elder at Grace Community Church in Tempe, Arizona

Bert and Jan: You have been faithfully discipling people for 50 years. Thank you for showing us and our family of eleven children (Jaime, Rachel, Casey, Megan, David, Nathan, Jason, Jacob, Abigail, Clara & Isaac) what it means to love God and to be controlled moment by moment by His Spirit. No two people have impacted us more for Christ! Couple of yielded bushes indeed!

Craig Rowland
Intel Development Engineer

About the Author

Bert Harned M.D.

Bert grew up in a Christian home in Kansas City, Missouri. He enjoyed playing football in high school, and was captain of the wrestling team when he attended Wheaton College in Illinois. He received his medical degree from Northwestern University Medical School and served his internship and anesthesia residency at Cook County Hospital in Chicago. He was certified by the American Board of Anesthesiology and practiced that specialty for forty years.

He married Jan in 1950. He then spent three and a half years in the United States Air Force as a flight surgeon in Greenland and Newfoundland. In 1979, he and Jan moved from Kansas City to the Phoenix area and retired from anesthesiology in 1988. He remains very active in church and in mentoring (discipling) mostly young married people. Along the way, he directed a Young Life club, and was on the associate staff of Campus Crusade for Christ. He also served as an elder and is currently a Sunday school teacher in his church.

Bert and Jan have two grown children and five grandboys who are spiritually strong. Bert loves flying and has a commercial pilot's license with instrument and instructor ratings, (and owned his own plane for some twenty years). Yet, he says that, "nothing is more exciting and motivating than the present privilege of helping young people who want to know God, and desire to be involved in His work."

Editor

Kerry L. Skinner, D.Min.

Kerry has served in pastoral roles for more than 30 years. He has co-authored books with Dr. Henry Brandt and Dr. Henry Blackaby.

Through his writing and teaching, Kerry is recognized internationally as an advocate of biblical sufficiency. He has conducted conferences for pastors, counselors, and lay leaders on biblical counseling, repentance, and holiness.

Kerry received his doctorate from Gordon-Conwell Theological Seminary with a focus on revival. A major portion of his study resulted in his latest book, *The Joy of Repentance*.

He and his wife, Elaine, have one son, Jason and three grandchildren.

Authored *The Joy of Repentance*, 2007
Co-authored *Wonderful Counselor: A Return to Truth* with Ab Abercrombie, 2007
Co-authored *Chosen to be God's Prophet* with Henry Blackaby, 2003
Co-authored *Called & Accountable* with Henry Blackaby, 2002
Co-authored *I Want to Enjoy My Children* with Henry Brandt, 2002
Co-authored *Created to be God's Friend* (workbook), with Henry Blackaby, 2000
Co-authored *Marriage God's Way*, with Henry Brandt, 1999
Co-authored *The Power of the Call*, with Henry T. Blackaby and Henry Brandt, 1997
Co-authored *The Heart of the Problem* (book and workbook), with Henry Brandt, 1995
Co-authored *The Word for the Wise* with Henry Brandt, 1995
Co-authored *Breaking Free from the Bondage of Sin* with Henry Brandt, 1994

www.kerryskinner.com

Foreword

The brilliant magenta sunset had just begun to fade on a warm Phoenix evening in February as Marianne and I walked slowly into the hotel ballroom. Glancing around the room, we saw a sea of couples seated at tables prepared for dinner.

The suspense in the room was mounting. We quietly slipped into our chairs and joined the well-dressed group of over two hundred people who were waiting for the special guests. An eerie silence permeated the ballroom as all four hundred eyes were glued to the door awaiting the entrance of Bert and Jan Harned.

Bert and Jan had spent their last five decades pouring their lives into the lives of others–introducing young and old to Jesus Christ–and then building relationships with them around God's Word. Their single purpose was unwavering–to bring everyone they touched into "full maturity in Jesus Christ."

The operating principle Bert and Jan have demonstrated for the past half century of discipleship is *availability*. They have been there for anyone who wants to know how to grow deeper with their LORD. And their home is always open.

I was one of those lives touched by their love and faithfulness. Fifty years ago, Bert, then a young anesthesiologist we called, "Doc," was my *Young Life* leader in Kansas City, Missouri. Bert and his lovely effervescent wife, Jan, spent hour upon hour living out Christ's love to me and other teens.

Bert and Jan enthusiastically taught me God's Word and helped me to understand the importance of living moment by moment for Christ. But they were also fun-loving, ordinary people. We went boating together, skiing together, eating together, laughing together, and taking trips together. The two of them were a living picture of what real Christianity is all about–and I got hooked!

Suddenly the large ballroom doors began to open. Bert and Jan's good friends, Dr. Henry Brandt and his wife Jo had invited them to a quiet dinner at the hotel. But what they thought would be a dinner suddenly erupted into a thunderous ovation as 200 grateful friends of Bert and Jan stood to honor their lives.

Bert and Jan froze. They stood motionless gazing around the room at faces so familiar. Bert was stunned–speechless at all the friends from across the country. Jan's face blossomed into a radiant smile of joy as she began waving to people she loved but hadn't seen for years.

Two hundred jubilant people, reflecting five decades of Bert and Jan's influence continued their applause as the two honored guests–so deeply touched by such an overwhelming expression of gratitude–tried to gain control of their emotions.

As the evening progressed, many testified of how God had used Bert and Jan to impact their lives for Christ. Each story was different and unique, but all seemed to carry the same thread of relationship building, modeling, discipling, and mentoring. Most of all–their continual availability.

Today in their early 80s, Bert and Jan Harned are still committed to changing lives. And they are still available! They work with singles and couples of all ages, hanging-out with them, and coaching them as they seek to grow in Christ. They delight in helping those stuck in the *chicken-yard of life* to soar like eagles.

Marianne and I are privileged to have observed New Testament discipleship firsthand with Bert and Jan. They are people who have taken God seriously–doing God's business His way. Both personally and with their marriage, they are simply being obedient to the Great Commission our Lord gave 2000 years ago.

After the evening festivities and testimonies were concluded, Marianne and I flew back to Seattle, pondering the impact of two lives totally sold out to Christ. We realized more than ever that Bert and Jan have invested their lives in us so that we in turn can invest ours in others. And that is what real discipleship is all about.

As you read through this book, perhaps you too will be challenged. As Bert often told me as a teen, "Life is short. Someday you will look back at your 70 to 80 years of life and be thankful for each day committed to Christ. You can make your life count for Him." And then with a twinkle in his eye he always reminded me,

Remember, any ole bush will do.

Larry Chapman
Businessman
Seattle, Washington

Preface

Becoming a disciple of Jesus Christ cannot simply be an addition to your full schedule. It is not a program that you participate in when you have time. The focus is not on doing things. Neither is the focus on community, small groups, core beliefs, or the church. The focus is "Jesus Christ and Him crucified" (1 Cor. 2:2). That is, to be in Christ and Him in you. "It is the Father, living in me, who is doing His work..." Those are the words of Jesus. Only God, through the control of His Holy Spirit, can transform you and me into His disciples. This is what I believe the emphasis of the teaching of the church should be–to make disciples. That is the focus of this book. It is not a simple matter. It requires personal investing of time, study, prayer, and submission by faith to all God shows us. It is not really a matter of more information. We have incredible reservoirs of information available to us. If knowledge could make us better, then we should be in excellent condition. Instead, we need to believe what we know and then to live daily in utter obedience, humility, and dependence on Him.

How long would it take for you to become a disciple? I believe a lot less than you think, and yet it takes a lifetime to complete.

Acknowledgements

Above all, I am more grateful than words can reveal for Jan, my wife of 59 years, who is always an encouragement to me, and many others. She is a brilliant example of a true godly wife.

Also, I am thankful for Terry Rossello and Jackie Pearson who spent a great deal of time proof-reading this book.

Chapter One
The Big Picture

The Chicken Yard

While soaring far above the earth one day, not very long ago, a majestic, far-sighted eagle decided to check out a chicken yard he had seen from his lofty place in the sky. So, he landed in the chicken yard. He found he could easily obtain food and water there, and after a bit, the chickens seemed to accept him. He decided to stay a spell–quite a while actually. He stayed so long he almost forgot he was an eagle!

He ate, and even began to enjoy, chicken food. The water was not like the clear, cold mountain streams he was used to, but it was freely available. He soon began to talk like a chicken, and to take on the value system that chickens embrace. And although the chicken wire fence was no problem for him, he stayed inside it just like the chickens did.

In fact, he began to like chickens and their ways, and thought that some day, he might marry a chicken and perhaps have chicken kids. He started going to chicken parties, enjoying chicken jokes, acting like a chicken, and lusting after good-looking chickens. He began to strut like chickens do. It didn't bother him too much that he was walking around in chicken doo all day and that he smelled like a chicken.

Any Ole Bush

He began to fear what chickens fear, and to get mad at what chickens get mad at, and even to be jealous of prosperous chickens. He got involved in many chicken activities, worked very long hours, expended much energy, often to the point of exhaustion, but–he really wasn't very happy there.

Now and then, he would glance up at the clear blue inviting sky, uneasily watching a fellow eagle soaring lazily in the sun. But then, he would put off the thought that he was missing a great deal, things like big-picture vision, freedom, and the flying fellowship–in fact, missing everything that he had been created to be. He had nearly forgotten what he was, his destiny, his dignity, and his sphere. He had deceived himself into believing he was having fun and was ignoring his gifts and talons (err–talents). He was wasting his life. If he stayed there, he would die a disillusioned, dirty bird with nothing that matters to report at his funeral.

You and I know this eagle would never be content in the chicken yard. He didn't belong there. He was pretending to be something he was not (that's the definition of a "hypocrite"). One day, he looked up into the beautiful clear sky and suddenly realized where he was, and what he was missing. He *repented* (changed his mind). He knew that he did not need bigger wings, or stronger wings, or more wings–he already had everything he needed. He simply needed to lift up his head, spread his beautiful wings and soar into the heavens–and he did.

Soaring is what the eagle was designed by his Creator to do and for which he is perfectly suited. The air is his element; it is natural for him to soar, to enjoy flying and have freedom from the pull of gravity. Like a car is designed by its maker to run on gas, and a pen is designed to use ink, so the eagle is designed to soar. The

The Big Picture

Christian is designed by God to be indwelt by God, the Holy Spirit, and to enjoy the beauty and pleasure of being guided and enabled by God Himself. A believer should delight in whatever God brings him each day. It is what is normal for him. To soar is not weird, odd, unusual, difficult, or complicated to an eagle, nor is it (in the spiritual sense) to the Christian. It is not just for a few *special eagles*, it is the normal life style for all eagles and by analogy for all believers who are "in Christ." Watchman Nee calls it *The Normal Christian Life*.

Why would a normal eagle (believer) not soar? Why would any eagle choose to stay in the chicken yard? Why would any Christian choose to live a selfish, carnal, self-centered, frustrated, angry, stressed life and never experience *normal*? It's hard to understand isn't it? I am afraid there are still a lot of eagles in the chicken yard!

> *Do not be yoked together with unbelievers..."Therefore come out from them and be separate," says the LORD. "Touch no unclean thing, and I will receive you. I will be a Father to you, and you will be my sons and daughters," says the LORD Almighty.*
>
> **2 Corinthians 6:14, 17-18**

> *Therefore, there is now no condemnation for those who are in Christ Jesus, because through Christ Jesus the law of the Spirit of life set me free from the law of sin and death.*
>
> **Romans 8:1-2**

> *In the same way, count yourselves dead to sin but alive to God in Christ Jesus. Therefore do not let sin reign in your mortal body so that you obey its evil desires.*
>
> **Romans 6:11-12**

Any Ole Bush

You cannot have *more*, and you do not need to have *less*.[1]

Major W. Ian Thomas

Fellow eagles–spread your wings. You can choose to be an eagle in the chicken yard and spend your life with the chickens–or you can soar!

Larry's Story: A Delightful Journey Out of the Chicken Yard

The summer sun was still very hot as I sat on the steps at the north door of Southwest High School waiting for my daily ride home from varsity football practice. Mom was never late, but that day, in August of 1958, she had completely forgotten me!

I had just sprained my ankle for the second time and it was swelling and hurting a great deal. What was I to do? It was just a week prior to the all important Shawnee Mission rivalry game and that ankle was going to undermine four years of intense sweaty practice, as well as far-fetched dreams of being a football hero.

The coach just would not understand, in fact, as a Christian Scientist he had mocked me four weeks before when I had sprained my ankle the first time. "It's all in your head," he said as he mockingly limped away.

I sat there utterly dejected, writhing in agony. All the other players were gone. Only the coaches remained in the locker room. Did I dare tell them about my ankle? No! I couldn't handle the torment of their mocking sarcasm and anger at me for letting them down just before the biggest game of the year.

As I considered my hopeless situation, I thought about my new relationship with Christ that was now approaching two years. My Young Life leader, Doc, had asked me three questions that jolted my thinking. "How did you get here? What are you doing here? Where are you going after you die?" It made me start thinking about the purpose of my life and prepared me for Doc's subsequent follow-up when I asked Christ to come into my life. I had good intentions to live a life pleasing to my Savior, but I

The Big Picture

had not made him LORD of my life. I was still deeply entrenched in myself, but at least now my life had purpose and meaning.

Doc and his lovely wife, Jan, had brightened up my life with their radiance of Christ's love and joy. As much as I wanted what they had, the pull of popularity and success at football was my main focus. I really wanted both. Maybe God would give me success at football so I could win others to Christ!

But now my dream of being a football hero had been crushed by an untimely injury. As I gave up hope of Mom picking me up, I cried out in desperation, "God help me!" I didn't really know what I was praying for, and did not expect an answer. At that point, I looked up in amazement and saw Doc driving toward me in his blue VW convertible. "Doc," I exclaimed as he drove up, "What are you doing here?"

"Well," he said, "I got off early at the hospital and just asked the LORD what He wanted me to do and felt that I should come over here and visit the football practice." I said, "I am really glad you are here. My ankle is killing me. I sprained it and I haven't told the coach yet because they don't believe in injuries. Would you mind telling them for me?"

"Let me see that ankle," he said. "That is a hum-dinger. You need to stay off it at least two weeks." "Two weeks!" I exclaimed. "Coach is going to have a fit." "Don't worry, I will talk to him," Doc said. I was greatly relieved as he walked down the west alley and into the locker room, but I still was devastated about missing the big game and knew it would be an uphill battle to restore the coach's confidence in me. Doc told the coach I would be out for two weeks. He came back to ask "Hey, do you need a lift home?" "You bet," I said. "There is no way I could walk home on this ankle."

As I hopped on one leg into the convertible, I reflected on the incredible way God had answered my prayer. Why did Doc get off early that day? Why did he get the impression to visit the football practice? Why did Mom forget to pick me up today? The only day she ever forgot! Why was I the only player still there *when Doc got there? As I thought about all of that, my faith was bolstered and a feeling of exhilaration came over me. In fact, the intense throbbing of my ankle suddenly lessened! I knew something special was happening. I felt almost like a spectator.*

"Hey Larry, I will be on call at the hospital the next two weeks (he was an anesthesiologist at St. Mary's Hospital in K.C.). You won't be able to practice. Why don't you come over to the hospital and we will have some time to chat." I really liked that idea. God had prepared my heart to soak up all that He had for me through Doc. The next two weeks were a turning point in my whole life as we poured over many things in the Scriptures and discussed what it meant to be a true disciple of Christ.

He said, "Larry, all these things you consider important like football, girls, popularity, and the like will not really matter 100 years from now. All that will be important is what you did for Jesus Christ. Your desire should be to please Him and make your life count for Him. That's what really matters." He taught me the importance of reading and memorizing the Word of God. He also emphasized the importance of prayer and Christian fellowship. I made some important commitments during that time that changed my life. What stands out the most is that when all is said and done, the only thing worth living for is Jesus Christ. I resolved to make my life count for Him.

Forty two years later, I am so thankful for those special life-changing times and the emphasis Doc put on purpose. To this day, we are the closest of friends and continue to encourage each other in our walk with God.

Larry is a successful businessman in Seattle. He has learned to soar. He has learned over the years what it means to deny self, to walk in the Spirit, and to let God be God in Him. It was Larry who first encouraged me to write this book with the purpose of helping people learn to see the big picture. Learning how to abide in Christ, and to live a normal, significant Christian life is our life purpose.

The Big Picture

The Big Picture

It was a hot summer day when we drove east from the Valley of the Sun. In less than three hours, we were "up on the rim" (a high bluff overlooking the whole Phoenix valley). High country above Phoenix is much cooler than the valley below. We camped there for a few days.

One day, I was sitting on the rim of a thousand-foot bluff overlooking the valley below. There were birds flying lazily in the summer sun. The view was beautiful and the temperature was perfect. I could see for seventy-five miles in three directions. The only distraction was a lot of flies.

I could see cars winding back and forth as they climbed up the mountain below my perch. I saw an accident that had completely stopped traffic. The cars below couldn't see the problem ahead. In that setting, I began to think about *the big picture*. I could see much more than the people in those cars could see. They were unknowingly approaching the accident. If they could only view what I was seeing, they could avoid the difficulty ahead. Yet, in terms of the really big picture of life, I too only have a small and limited view.

Those flies were incredibly distracting! I would sit and think great and lofty thoughts about God and the future, about purpose and meaning–then I would swat a couple flies. I thought about the fact that God is, and He knows, and He is sovereign, He owns and runs it all–and swat three or four more flies.

I thought of the privilege of knowing God personally, of being part of His family and being loved by Him. I pondered how I was guided by His indwelling Holy Spirit, that I am dead to sin and alive to God, and that He gives me–SWAT–everything I need for life and godliness. I remembered how Hebrews 13:5 (AMP) says that God will never leave me, "[I will] not, [I will] not, [I will] not in any degree leave you helpless nor forsake nor let [you] down (relax My hold on you)! [Assuredly not!]"

An even bigger picture is Jonathan Edwards' book, *The End for Which God Created the World*. I agree with his profound and magnificent conclusion that the end of everything–God's purpose for all creation–is to bring glory to God. *That* is the big picture. Swat, swat, swat.

There was a big hawk effortlessly floating on the updrafts in front of me–a really beautiful sight. It reminded me of God's incredible creation. A hummingbird was whirring around close to my perch. I also noticed that there was a tremendous amount of trash there. Maybe it was left by previous *big picture* thinkers.

I thought of how Jesus Christ loved me so much that He died in my place, for my sins, and that His desire is for me to be in heaven with Him, forever. Incredible! But then, there was all that trash, and flies–swat!

I have peace with God, and I also have the peace of God. Also, Hebrews 13:5 says "Never will I leave you; never will I forsake you." Isaiah 41:10 says, "So do not fear, for I am with you; do not be dismayed, for I am your God." I am therefore, never without a source of wisdom, joy, and love. That is the kind of thinking that sets you free. Fabulous!

I think I learned that life is always going to have many kinds of distractions and annoying trash and flies. I can choose at any moment of my day to swat flies and sputter about trash, or I can choose to focus my thinking at that moment on the incredibly lofty, satisfying truth of God.

So the "Big Picture" for a Christian is to abide in Christ, to be controlled by His Spirit and to let Him live His life in me.

My Story: How God Led Me Into Discipling

When I realized that Christ was in my life and would live His life through me, I began to teach Sunday school and Bible studies. Witnessing to people about their need of a personal relationship

The Big Picture

with Christ also became an active part of my life. My wife and I became involved in the *Young Life* ministry for several years and later with *Campus Crusade for Christ* where we learned a great deal more about how to walk in the Spirit, and how to lead others to Christ.

Wanting to see God work in greater depth and power in people's lives, God helped me to focus on the idea of *discipling* people. If I could teach them, then they would, "be qualified to teach others" (2 Tim. 2:2). Billy Graham realized that for his evangelistic ministry to have lasting change in his converts, that there had to be significant ongoing teaching and personal follow-up. At a conference one summer, I was challenged by the speaker, Charles Stanley, to go home and find some men who wanted to be men of God. He encouraged me to meet with them over an extended period of time and teach these men to be controlled by the Holy Spirit. That was exactly what I wanted to do.

Although I was working full-time as an anesthesiologist, I challenged twenty men in my church to meet every week for fellowship and accountability. Their assignment was to spend one hour a day doing what was assigned in Bible study, memorization, and the reading of great books. Amazingly, they all came! That was the beginning, some fifty years ago. I soon learned that you cannot disciple that many men at once. My wife and I also learned that the wives wanted to be included. We shifted from discipling just men, to couples. Couples growing simultaneously is best for the home. We normally resist meeting with just one spouse and encourage them to wait until their spouse would join the group. We meet with a number of singles as well. Working full-time prevented us from meeting with more than four or five couples at a time. Now, as a retired M.D., my wife and I are able to meet with about twelve to fifteen people on a regular basis.

ANY OLE BUSH

In the following chapters, we will share some biblical methods of discipleship we have found very practical and useful. But before we go any further, remember, God can do anything He wants through any surrendered person. Any person *will do* when Christ lives and works *through* them. It is not the bush, but what the bush contains that is important.

---

[1] Major W. Ian Thomas, *The Saving Life of Christ*, (Grand Rapids, Michigan: Zondervan, 1961), 70.

Chapter Two
A Disciple–A Bush on Fire

One day, Moses, one of the most important men in the Bible, was walking through the hot sand on the back side of the desert (Exod. 3). God's audible voice gave him his life task. God spoke to him out of a burning bush–not *the* bush, not just *a* bush...*any* ole bush would do. There was nothing special or magical or supernatural about the bush. What made it special was that God was in it. (paraphrasing Major W. Ian Thomas).

That is a picture of every believer. There is nothing special about believers, we look like all the other bushes (believers) but there is an enormous difference between what any ole bush can do, as compared with any ole bush that contains God. It's not the bush, but what the bush contains. Jesus said,

> *"...it is the Father, living in me, who is doing his work."*
>
> **John 14:10**

That's it!! When you understand that statement, everything is simplified and focused–it becomes not only real, but possible to everyone–to you! You can condense it all down to one word–*IN*, that is–Christ *IN* you.

HOW shall we then live? The Scripture has a magnificent answer to that question:

> *...that you may be filled [through all your being] unto all the fullness of God [may have the richest measure of the divine*

Any Ole Bush

Presence, and become a body wholly filled and flooded with God Himself]!

Eph. 3:19, AMP

I am earnestly seeking to help others understand how this marvelous filling, flooding, and enabling of the Holy Spirit can be practical and real. Although it is necessary to know what the Bible says about it all, in the end it is very uncomplicated and simple! God wants everyone to understand this simple, but profound truth of the Christian life!

A person who is earnest about being a serious disciple of Christ cannot be proud, disobedient, selfish, immoral, impatient, or unkind. Jesus said to "Go and make disciples." Can anybody be a disciple? Yes, but only as you are controlled by the Holy Spirit.

Are you a person who is tired of mediocrity, fears, failure, fruitlessness, uncertainty, worry, frustration, struggling, discouragement, doubts, and boredom? If so, welcome aboard! There is a glorious yet simple biblical solution. It is personal, practical, available today, and best of all it is God's doing–His plan. All we have to do is accept it, by faith. Jesus *nailed it* when He said, "...it is the Father, living in me, who is doing his work."

Church attendance, singing in the choir, being an elder, a Sunday school teacher, a pastor, giving money, joining a small group, going on mission trips, or any and all of these together (good, commendable, necessary things) *do not make you a disciple*!

Investing two hours per week in Bible study and prayer, and twenty-five hours per week watching TV, plus five more hours reading magazines, newspapers, and many more hours in sports events, concerts, picnics and the like is not the balance you need. Although there is some value in all of these, your purpose is to be a *disciple* and glorify God with your life.

A Disciple–A Bush on Fire

The Two Most Important Things
1. To walk in the Spirit (Abide in Christ)
2. To make disciples

That is the focus and goal of this writing–to elevate, illuminate, make clear, delineate, and clarify God's plan for helping a person to be controlled by the Spirit. We call that process *discipling*. How do we best do that? The essential, non-optional requirement is that you abide in Christ; that is, that you are controlled by the Holy Spirit in daily life. A disciple seeks to bring glory to God, seeks only God's will, and intends to bring every thought captive to Christ.

John: A Burning Bush Example

John was a singles pastor when we met him and his wife. He called us one day to talk about discipleship. We explained that we would like to meet with both of them. Through our visit, we discovered that we had tennis in common. Often before our discipleship meeting, we would play tennis. His wife and my wife, Jan, became good friends. This eventually led John's wife to a women's Bible study at our church.

We met with both of them for about two years. God was preparing John to become the discipleship pastor at a church in another state. As we met each week, we talked about many issues and gave them reading assignments. They were faithful to read many impacting books, studies, verses, and study biblical principles.

Many personal needs surfaced in John as we talked and prayed together. He discovered marriage problems, lust problems, motivation difficulties, time management needs, and his need for accountability. He stated that he was really "tired–exhausted actually."

John did not have a physical problem. He was healthy and strong. His problem was both emotional and mental. Stress and pressure had become his major problem. John knew biblical doctrine, but he was trying to operate in the flesh. He had not yet come to understand that the fruit of the Spirit is not stress and exhaustion, but rather it is joy, peace, contentment, and love. I suggested that every week for the next two months he take time for a half day of prayer and time alone with the Lord!

I made notes of all our meetings and found I had twenty-three pages of notes regarding him! From these notes, I realized that we had covered many important issues and discussed many books. We had read Gary Inrig's *Excellence*, Henry Drummond's *Greatest Thing in the World*, James Stalker's *Life of St Paul*, Charles Spurgeon's *Lectures to My Students*, Steven Charnock's *Existence and Attributes of God*, Major W. Ian Thomas's *Saving Life of Christ*, and *Mystery of Godliness*. It is my firm conviction that reading the Bible and reading great books is an absolute necessity for the one who wants to be a godly person.

We also discussed what *success* looks like from God's point of view, the need for vision, consistency, and excellence. We spent time dealing with his problem of lust and God's adequate answer for such constant temptation. This issue needs to be addressed for John (a future pastor) and all believers. This terrible cancer of immorality is unrelentingly served up to us (pastors included!) by all the media.

We talked about the need for worship, prayer, time in God's Word, and memorizing God's Word. We spent time studying the marvelous truth that God loves us. This is one of the deepest wells of motivational truth in the Bible!

Jan was meeting with his wife during this same time. Reports, from her point of view as to John's spiritual progress, were very interesting. She said, "He was a good husband this week." Yet, in my notes he said, "Not so good this week. She was overreacting. I did not handle it well, but we worked through it." In real life, that is

A Disciple–A Bush on Fire

where "the rubber meets the road." The next week, my notes on John stated, "Husbanding this week, very good. It helped to think of God's love for her through me."

We spent time going over how to proceed with some men he began discipling. We talked about handling financial matters, time management, and "can you really trust God no matter what?" That is a very big issue! We talked about obedience, keeping his weight in check, and getting enough exercise. I let him know that I had very high expectations of what God would do with him.

Jan and I also address *purpose* with potential disciples, since that is an exceedingly important foundation for everyone. Most people have never discovered their life purpose. John said his life purpose was "to have my group grow and for me to be a senior pastor some day."

My response was, "And then what? Senior pastor is a position I am sure you will attain. That is an objective, not a purpose. A better purpose might be 'to be a godly man.' If that is your purpose, then you can determine what is *vital* in order to get there. What is vital is different for one who wants to be a godly man as opposed to one who wants to be president of a large company. The coach of a swimming team would have a different program for a swimmer who wanted to be able to swim the width of the pool, in contrast to a swimmer who wanted to win the Olympics."

We met at home, at his office, on the tennis court, and sometimes in the car. Seem like a lot of meetings? It was, but as Gary Inrig said, "All excellence involves discipline and tenacity of purpose."[1] My conviction is that it takes time secluded from a zillion other things to give God a chance to change your thinking. That is our part, to give God our time and attention.

John is currently a pastor with a productive discipling ministry! Here is a wonderful letter he wrote some six years after our discipling time together:

ANY OLE BUSH

Dear Bert,

In the last couple of months, you have been on my mind. Right now, I'm discipling three guys. As I've worked with them, I have been so appreciative of your building into my life. There are a number of ways that you really helped me grow spiritually.

You really challenged me to know Christ in an intimate way. Philippians 3:10, "For my determined purpose is that I might know Him…that I may progressively become more deeply and intimately acquainted with Him, perceiving and recognizing and understanding (the wonders of His person) more strongly and more clearly." You had me meditate on this verse and it showed me Paul's passion for knowing Christ.

You had me meditating on verses that talk about God's character. First of all, you taught me to meditate and reflect on what the verse was saying to me. You would have me take a verse and think about it for 10 to 15 minutes. As I meditated on Isaiah 49:15-16, Isaiah 43:1-4, and Jeremiah 31:5 and many more, God really spoke to me. You also gave me a copy of your own journaling as you meditated on God's love. That was helpful to see how you interacted with Scripture and how God spoke to you.

These have been foundations for my life. I have continued to meditate on God's character and seek to know Him. That has deeply impacted me. I think of Ephesians 3:16-21 where it talks about experiencing God to the fullest, being strengthened in my inner man, and being filled to all the fullness of God. As I have reflected on God's love, I have seen this happen.

The Lost Art of Disciple Making by Leroy Eims, was a great book you suggested to give me a heart for disciple making. It was very helpful to understand what discipleship is all about.

One of the other things was that you had me memorizing a number of verses. You were teaching me to put God's Word into my heart. Right now, I am using the Navs 2:7 course with one of the guys I am discipling. Your life and what you modeled to me made a big impact. You spent an hour a day with God and you

A Disciple–A Bush on Fire

kept a journal. I remember that. I don't remember journaling much before you discipled me, but I have been pretty faithful over the last eight years to journal in my quiet times. In my quiet times, I try to spend a good amount of time with the Lord, not to rush in and get out. You taught me to quiet myself before God and to listen to Him, and to pray. All of that takes time. You also modeled the importance of disciple making and that rubbed off on me as well.

The God You Can Know by Dan DeHaan was a great book. It taught me to know Christ deeper and to spend time with Him and I have used it with others.

Bert, thanks so much for what you have given to me, which is a deeper walk with the Lord. I now know Him, really know Him. Thanks for that gift!

I am trusting that you, like John, want to live out John 14:10–to know God intimately. If you intend to live for Him instead of self, and to teach others to do the same, read on! These thoughts will be of great interest to Christians who are tired of playing church, tired of mediocrity; weary of living with little meaning, excitement and purpose, and bearing little fruit. Though you are serious about pleasing God, you may still be struggling with unwanted sins, attitudes, fears, worries, anger and selfishness. I pray you have come to the point of being willing to pay the cost of denying self, giving up your rights, and being counted as one of His.

What is Required?
1. A mind set based on Scripture.
2. Your will must be replaced with God's Will.
3. You must know you are dead to sin and alive to God.
4. Understand how to continually abide in Christ, and walk in the Spirit.

Part of living up to the requirements of discipleship involves replacing wasted time with things that are pleasing to God. Like what? (Now it's going to get interesting!) Here are some ideas:

Any Ole Bush

1. Would you agree that the great majority of TV and its advertising certainly does not glorify God?
2. Most magazines, newspapers, and the like have very little that honors God.
3. Sports events, games, concerts, picnics, biking, hiking, climbing, and bull riding....replaced by something better. For example, replace golf with something that doesn't take half a day.
4. Good books....although interesting, rob you of reading the best of Christian classics, and the Bible.
5. Spiritual activities that do not contribute to God's plan for you.
6. Hollywood movies certainly do not deepen your perception of a loving and sovereign God.
7. If it is not essential to your abiding in Christ–why do you do it?

In real life, that translates into a willingness to drop potent usurpers. Sports, games, hobbies, endless meetings, multiple activities, or perhaps even your job, can rob you of intimacy with God. Intimacy with Him results from spending a considerable amount of time in His Word. Accountability to someone close to you helps you to stay on target with your daily time in the Word. Sharing with others the amount of time you read, pray, and think is a part of discipleship. Willingness to be rebuked, corrected, and instructed by others reveals a teachable spirit.

Plan to spend your vacations in a way that will be spiritually helpful and encouraging instead of perhaps lolling on a beach with lots of people who do not care one thing about honoring God. Can you honor God while enjoying the beach experience? Of course! (I have been there!) What matters in all this is your intent. Your life purpose is to glorify and enjoy God.

A Disciple–A Bush on Fire

A very large issue is learning to be obedient to all that God says, in every area of your life. (That is a "biggee") It is obvious that you cannot be controlled by the Holy Spirit while living in disobedience to His commands and will. (See Chapter Six)

---

[1] Gary Inrig, *A Call to Excellence*, (Wheaton, Illinois, Victor Books, 1985), 103.

Any Ole Bush

Chapter Three
The 1-ON-1: Our Game Plan

Is there a curriculum? Well, sorta...

Bill says, "I want to learn to swim the length of the pool." Joe says, "I want to win a gold Olympic swimming medal." The curriculum requirement for Bill would be different than for Joe. We want to develop a program for the likes of Joe.

The 1-ON-1 is a loose leaf workbook containing 12 lessons involving study, lists of Scripture, recommended reading, memory verses, testimony writing, and the meeting of current needs. When we start a discipling relationship, it begins with studying through the 1-ON-1 notebook together. Allowing for breaks, illnesses, vacations, emergencies, family visits, forgetfulness and the like, it can take a year or more. Meetings are scheduled every other week to go over the assigned lesson. The study has a flexible schedule, but strong personal accountability. The curriculum developed largely out of our experience with *Campus Crusade for Christ*, the *Navigators*, and *Walk Thru the Bible* ministries. Over the years, we have continued to modify and improve it with the objective of making disciples.

1-ON-1 discipleship curriculum is available to anyone who wants to use it. It is on my web page, *www.bertsgoodstuff.com* in the form of downloadable Adobe PDF files. Many of the people we disciple download and print this material when they begin to disciple their friends.

Any Ole Bush

Before starting, we are very *up front* and *clear* about what we expect in terms of time and commitment. We want to see strong desire, conviction, intensity, and purpose in the heart of a potential disciple. Commitment is essential. We expect them to be reliable, which simply means they will do the work, and be at the meetings. Discipleship does not happen in a half-hearted environment. Someone said, "Don't hold hands with the half-hearted." A disciple should want to use not only a few hours a week of his time, but all of his time to please God. He believes it is vital to spend time in prayer, Bible study, reading, memorizing, and fellowship with others who intend to be disciples of Jesus.

Jan and I believe it is not only helpful, but essential, to be exposed to great men of God whenever possible. We seek out those opportunities. One example is when Dr. Henry Brandt came to our town. We invited some couples to have dinner with him. The dinner resulted in some quality time with Dr. Brandt. We watched God use him to produce real life change in several couples with just one evening of casual fellowship. It has been correctly said that you never want to listen to just one voice. Exposing these disciples to great men of God by way of conferences, personal meetings, tapes, books, and videos is worthwhile.

In real life, these requirements for discipleship mean that some activities must be dropped in order to free up the necessary time. Some things will be diminished or left out, such as television, movies, hobbies, committee meetings, and sporting events. As difficult as this may be, there must be vision, commitment, and self-discipline or discipleship will not happen. When inevitable pressures come, without strong commitment, the spiritual priorities are the first to go. Discipleship requires a major shift of focus, a whole different mindset–not an addition to your already full plate. But the reward is enormous.

1-ON-1: Our Game Plan

Discipling involves not only teaching, but doing things together. Hiking, camping, tennis, and picnics are some of the ways to develop true Christian fellowship. Being an example, being available, and making phone calls to one another are a part of the process. We become close friends and get to know real needs, failures, and hopes. We encourage, challenge, and reprove each other and continue to meet as long as is needed. Sometimes we meet for only a few months, but often for many years. Our objective is to see our friend become strong in faith, learn how to feed himself from the Word of God, and be equipped to be an outlet of God's truth and love–able to teach others. In short, a *reproducer*. The Scripture makes it clear:

> *And the things you have heard me say in the presence of many witnesses entrust to reliable men who will also be qualified to teach others.*
>
> **2 Timothy 2:2**

That…is discipling!

- Witnessing without discipling lasts only one generation.
  - Discipling reproduces into succeeding generations.
    - The heart of "the Great Commission" is "making disciples."

Matthew 16:33

1-ON-1: A Short Overview of the 12 Lessons

Lesson One: Be Sure

How To Be Sure You Are A Christian is the focus of this study. We always study this chapter with everyone for two reasons. First, to be sure they really know Christ as their personal Savior and know how to substantiate that with Scripture. This study addresses who

Any Ole Bush

Jesus is, how He died for our sins, and how to know Him as your personal Savior. Second, they need to know how to effectively teach someone else these truths. This chapter has been used by some to lead their friends to Christ.

Lesson Two: The Holy Spirit

This is the most important area of study for a believer, but it is not well understood. Clarifying how the Christian is filled and controlled by the Holy Spirit is critical for discipleship. Many good books and articles have been written about this vital teaching. My main motivation for writing this book is to make clear, focus, reveal, and shed light on this main issue of the Christian life. Jesus clearly explained it when He said:

> ...it is the Father, living in me, who is doing his work.
>
> **John 14:10**
>
> ...your will be done on earth as it is in heaven.
>
> **Matthew 6:10**

Oh, that we could learn to live with that mindset! It takes time to gain factual knowledge. Scriptural knowledge about the Holy Spirit, as well as God's love and plans for us are foundational truths. Accurate thinking requires accurate facts. Relentless study of the Scripture is essential. When you know what God says in the Bible, then it is very simple to let Christ live His life in you. It is a matter of faith in a God who cannot lie. It is not complicated, yet it is not easy. It is not easy, but neither is it out of reach. It is God's plan for every believer. It is the normal thing and it is the main thing. God has planned for everyone to know and experience this marvelous life which comes out of a biblical mindset and results in a lifestyle that honors God.

Part of the assignment in this lesson is to read and memorize 2 Corinthians 5:17. It is one thing to know (to be in possession of

1-ON-1: Our Game Plan

these truths) and it is quite another to be under their influence. Is it possible to be in possession of a bottle of wine (Eph 5:17) and not be under its influence? Certainly! To be under the influence you have to drink it! That is something that you choose to do or choose to ignore.

In some ways, it is like learning to drive a car. There is a great deal of knowledge required to drive a car. Learning traffic laws is essential, but it is also necessary to learn the basic functions and mechanisms of the car. You learn all this little by little, and after a while, it becomes second nature. You no longer have to study the laws or details of the car to drive. Driving becomes essentially automatic because you already know what you need in order to drive.

<u>Reading</u> <u>Assignment</u>: *The Saving Life of Christ,* by Major W. Ian Thomas.

Lesson Three

Studying God's attributes helps us know Him. When our mind is focused on God's character, we will be able to develop our relationship with Him through spiritual eyes and ears. Seeing and hearing about God's infinitely wonderful character helps us realize how we can experience His love and joy. That is why we teach how to WITS first (walk in the Spirit), and then one can grasp other things.

BELIEF CAUSES BEHAVIOR
Therefore, it is vital to be certain of our facts.

Some say, "What you think determines what you do." The Bible tells us that what you believe determines what you do. Science tells us that every input to our minds–sticks. Therefore, there is an enormous growing pool of information in your mind, most of which is subconscious. What you think is what really matters. Picture your mind as a huge *vat* with two big pipes pouring into it everything you hear, see, smell, read, and experience. One is the world's point of view, and the other is God's. You determine how much each pipe contributes to your *vat*, but the world has a huge amount of information coming in automatically each day! Your thoughts, values, anger, decisions, beliefs, fears, joy, and attitudes are all by-products of what is in there! There are enormous ramifications! Remember that Tozer said in one of his books that "the most important thing about anyone, is what you think when you think about God."[1] Since you want to think right about God, you need the correct information (i.e. what the Bible says) in your *vat*. How much do you receive from God's Word daily?

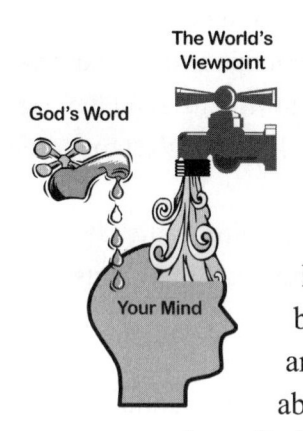

All of us contaminate our *vat* (mind), which is like putting dirt in a glass of water! The dirt might sink to the bottom of the glass, but it is still there. If the water is stirred, it will bring the dirt to the surface again. The mind can also be stirred to bring to a conscious level what has been stored there. For example, we may have much good information in our minds about God and truth, and then someone tells us a dirty story. Both are now in the mind! We could let it sink to the bottom, or we could stir it up and think about it. We have to make those choices every day.

A distorted, inaccurate view of God will result in a distorted, inaccurate response to Him! God's Word is the place to get the right stuff. What does God reveal about Himself in the Bible? Plenty!! He is eternal. He had no beginning and no end. Nothing existed before Him. No one created Him. Nothing is difficult for Him. He created all the universe, with all the elements and the laws to control it by simply willing it! He is everywhere all at once. He does not move! He does not change, grow, develop, or learn. He knows all that can be known. He hates sin and loves righteousness. He is never surprised, never has to ask questions, never discovers anything, and does not seek information. He has total knowledge and infinite wisdom to apply it. He is absolutely holy. In addition to all that, He is infinitely loving, kind, patient, and gracious! How's that for some good stuff for your *vat*!

When I studied to become an anesthesiologist, I needed to have correct data in my *vat*. How did I get it? Mostly by reading and listening to experienced anesthesiologists. The practice of anesthesiology is a matter of making lots of decisions, some of which are obviously critical. These decisions are made on the basis of what is in the *vat*. I could not use what was not there!

<u>Reading</u> <u>Assignment</u>: *The Knowledge of The Holy*, A. W. Tozer; and *The God You Can Know*, Dan DeHaan.

Lesson Four

The Bible is the only source of truth about God's thinking, ways, plans, desires, and character. Everything we know about Him is in the Bible. You cannot get God's mindset from TV!! Everyone knows that! You don't get it from school, or newspapers, or the media. It is not to be found on the beach at Waikiki, or even hiking in the woods in the moonlight (nothing wrong with that of course). You sure don't hear it at football games, or in the locker rooms, or in corporate offices. Where then can you get God's view of reality? It's a no-brainer, isn't it? You get it from three places:

First: Reading the Bible.

Second: Reading great books written by those who have invested large, quality chunks of time reading, studying, memorizing, and meditating on God's written Word.

Third: Intimate fellowship with those who spend time in places one and two!

<u>Reading</u> <u>Assignment</u>: *The Stranger on the Road to Emmaus*, by John R. Cross.

Any Ole Bush

Lesson Five

There is a shameful need for believing prayer in the church today. I am convinced that most believers don't really believe what God says about prayer! Developing a prayer notebook is highlighted in this lesson. Also, many verses are studied concerning why we pray, and how and to Whom we pray.

Lesson Six

Christian fellowship is examined in this lesson. The family of believers, (the church) is studied as we read and outline 1 John, and memorize Romans 12:4-5.

Reading Assignment: *Fresh Wind Fresh Fire* by Jim Cymbala.

Lesson Seven

Witnessing, sharing the good news, and how to help a person come to salvation by faith in Jesus Christ is the focus of this lesson. The *Four Spiritual Laws* booklet is introduced. A short study of Philippians is suggested, and Matthew 4:19 is assigned for memorization.

Reading Assignment: *Share Jesus Without Fear* by William Fay, and *More Than a Carpenter* by Josh McDowell.

Lesson Eight

Obedience and how to handle inevitable temptations is the focus of this lesson. We work on the memorization of 1 Corinthians 10:13. Walking in the Spirit will not tolerate disobedience in daily living.

Reading Assignment: *Grace Rules* by Steve McVey.

Lesson Nine

The all important subject of God's plan for marriage is introduced in this lesson. Next to the decision resulting in salvation, and the submission of our will to the control of the Holy Spirit, this is the most important decision any person makes in this life!

1-ON-1: Our Game Plan

If we know that a couple is having some marital problems, we sometimes start with this lesson in order to meet immediate needs. However, we always refer back to lesson two in order to help everyone realize the unrelenting necessity of being empowered by the Holy Spirit, especially when it comes to a healthy, godly marriage. That is the bottom line!

Lesson Ten

Godly parenting–how desperately it is needed! Terrible consequences follow its absence. The basic issue at stake is submission to authority. This lesson contains some outstanding material and valuable references. We know from a great deal of personal experience and observation that many (most?) Christian parents are woefully lacking in how to raise godly children. It is an enormous tragedy.

At a national law enforcement meeting a few years ago, it was concluded that the most dangerous thing in our country was the "lack of respect for authority."

Reading Assignment: *Shepherding a Child's Heart* by Ted Tripp.

Lesson Eleven

This lesson is called "How to Make Disciples." As in all these lessons, the real objective is application, not accumulation of information. Many practical suggestions are included. A list of recommended books follows.

My website: **www.bertsgoodstuff.com** contains the entire 1-ON-1 plan. Free downloadable PDF files are available for the lessons.

Meetings

We usually plan to meet every other week. We suggest meeting at our home. If a couple has small children, we suggest going to their house, so we can meet with them after the children are in bed. We have not found restaurants to be a good meeting place.

Any Ole Bush

A few years ago, we became friends with a graduate student going to Arizona State University in the Phoenix area. Although he was a Buddhist, he started coming to our Sunday school class. He would bring his English/Chinese dictionary to look up unfamiliar words! He was eager to learn about Jesus and the Christian faith. Along the way, he accepted Christ as his personal Savior, but soon thereafter moved to another state to begin his career. We only had time before he moved to simply introduce him to the 1-ON-1. For the next two years, we would talk with him by phone, along with his new (Christian) wife every other Saturday evening to go over their lesson. These meetings worked beautifully. They soon joined a strong, Bible-believing church, had a family, and we are still great long-distance friends. In fact, one year they spent Christmas with us in Phoenix.

Our typical meetings last for about an hour and a half. We go over the assigned lesson together, talk about the content, ask questions, and talk about what is currently important to them. Asking questions and going over the material often reveals problems, troubles, or questions that are sometimes completely outside the lesson. We usually separate the men and women for part of the time so that Jan spends time with the wife, and I with the husband. This allows for some interesting discussion!

Once a couple came to our house on a motorcycle. I went over the lesson and some other stuff with the husband. Jan, in a separate room, did the same with the wife. The wife had a master's degree in special education. The husband had a very interesting background which included some time as a hippie, but had no college background. They were attending church and he was even teaching a high school Sunday school class. After they left, Jan asked me, "Did he mention the terrible fight they had on the way to meet us?" He had not mentioned one word of it to me! I knew nothing of what had

1-ON-1: Our Game Plan

been a huge problem to them! This was early in our meetings with that couple, and they were both pretty new believers. Jan said that in their discussion, she had shocked Jan by volunteering, "It's no problem, if things don't go well, I'll just divorce him." I am happy to say that they have turned out to be one of the really strong and stable families in our church!

The husband of another couple started meeting with me. His wife told Jan she didn't like him spending all that time with me. And doing his homework at home cut into the time he could spend with her. It was causing friction and separating them. She and Jan talked about this, and soon we began meeting together as couples. They started growing together spiritually and have become strong and mature. They have a solid, godly marriage today and are influencing many others for Christ. We love it!

We tell folks repeatedly that the goal is not to finish the material, but to *get it*, that is, to grasp what God wants them to know. It is a process that takes time. How many weeks do we meet? It varies; sometimes just long enough to finish the 1-ON-1, but usually we go on to study *The Heart of The Problem* by Henry Brandt and Kerry L. Skinner. We also may study a book of the Bible, or a specific topic. We have several couples with whom we are still meeting more or less regularly after more than 10 years!

We have had a few (but thankfully, very few) who faded away after a few meetings. Scripture indicates that there is such a thing as seed falling on poor ground. So we accept that and move on.

Where Do We Find Potential Disciples?

Many come from our church activities such as Sunday school. Some come from the friendship of previously discipled folks. Jean said this about a couple of her friends:

Any Ole Bush

Debbie had been a Christian for ten years. She was yearning for a woman who could help her study and understand God's Word. When I met her, we were new to the state and attended the same church as she and her family. We talked a number of times and enjoyed one another's company. She had helped me a few times by watching the kids. I wanted to thank her, but, with something that would make a difference in her life. Tim (my husband) agreed with my desire to give her and her husband copies of the 1-ON-1 as a thank you. She called me the next day and asked if I would take her through the study. I told her to ask her husband first (exactly what Jan had taught me). Well, she said her husband agreed to our meeting and type of study. She actually cried with thankfulness for the chance to finally be discipled. She was an excellent student of the LORD and His Word and there were so many drastic changes within our first three weeks of study that her husband asked if my husband would take him through the study too! They have referred many times to the difference in their lives because they got the chance to read, study, ask, be prayed for, and be shown how wonderful Jesus is.

Helen is Chinese and had finally received permission to come to live in the United States, joining her husband. She was struggling with how to be a godly wife, mother, and child of God in a new land. She was in her last two months of pregnancy when she met Jan at church. Jan could relate to her culture shock of a new country because of her own background (her parents being from Germany). Jan learned that for many months, Helen had a desire to study with another woman, but no one had come forward and she thought "the LORD didn't have anyone for me." After getting to know each other for about four months, she asked if Jan would

1-ON-1: Our Game Plan

study with her. They attempted one study, but since it did not meet her needs, they shifted to the 1-ON-1. They went over parts of the lesson a little at a time. Instead of going through the material at a steady pace, they took time to read, talk, talk, talk, and refer back to the material many times. Jan knew that discipling someone requires going at their pace, being sensitive to their need, and waiting for the Holy Spirit's guidance."

Others are discovered with an interest in discipleship from speaking to small groups. I spoke one Sunday for another church's Sunday school group and one of the men there heard me mention how trusting the artificial horizon in the plane (the instrument that shows the altitude of the plane) was the same kind of faith one uses to trust God. I was flying my own plane from Kansas City to Omaha that afternoon to help with a Billy Graham meeting. He was very interested in flying and asked if he could go along. Our conversation included how I had become a Christian back in college. I also discovered that he had very little knowledge of the Gospel. I gave him a book about the "Uniqueness of Jesus." We stayed in touch. In a few weeks, he called to tell me he had accepted Christ as his personal Savior! His wife became a believer a few weeks later. We began to help them grow, not so much in regular meetings, but in casual fellowship, making suggestions, and praying together.

After we moved to Arizona, their family visited us and we took them for a jeep ride in the desert one day. His son, sitting in the back seat of the Jeep said to me, "You know what–you are my spiritual grandfather! You led my dad to Christ, and he led me to Christ."

We stayed in touch off and on for the next thirty plus years! A few years ago, he died suddenly while on a vacation trip. He lived a life of love and service to others and to his family. We received a letter from his wife a couple months after the memorial service. She told us she had received hundreds of letters from all over the coun-

Any Ole Bush

try relating how he had helped people in so many ways. He had shared the gospel with a great many (500) of them!

Is that "good stuff" or what!!?

Many have heard about 1-ON-1 discipleship from previous satisfied customers. Tim heard about us from a mutual friend who was interested in growing spiritually. We arranged to have lunch together. As we got acquainted, I asked about his prayer time, Bible reading and the like. He told me he was very busy with work and family. He said he really had little time for those things but did go to church occasionally. So, I casually suggested he was not serious about knowing God or about spiritual growth–and probably would not want to get into the 1-ON-1 just now.

I learned later he did not like that remark at all, but it made him think. Later, he and his wife did a great job of studying with us through the 1-ON-1. Today (many years later), he has a great family, is very active in church, and has discipled others also. They definitely qualify for the title of *disciples*! When someone says they just "don't have time right now," we suggest waiting until they do.

Betty Jo met a mutual friend of ours in a weight-loss class who talked with her about discipling. She wanted to be discipled, but the friend just didn't have the time to do it, and called us to see if Jan could disciple her. We again wanted to know if her husband would be interested in doing the same. She realized he was probably way too busy with his computer design work. He is a "type A", efficient, hard worker. She talked to him about her desire for them to be discipled together, and waited until he was ready. Eventually, they both responded. He responded very positively, and grew rapidly in faith and in intimacy with God. We had nearly a year of interaction and growing together before his job took him to another state. They both felt that the time with us was God's preparation for them. Ten years later, we still keep in touch with them through email. Their marriage is doing well, and so are their children.

1-ON-1: Our Game Plan

George and Mary, a newly married couple, came to our Sunday school class. He was working on his CPA and she was near a master's in mechanical engineering. I talked to him about the need for them to be discipled together, but he felt she was too busy and would feel unable to do it at that time. They talked and she thought she would like to try it, so we started meeting. Jan met with the wife and I with the husband. She started memorizing some verses about salvation as we worked together. She received news that her father was dying of cancer and had only a few weeks to live. They went to see him, and shared the verses just memorized about how to be sure of salvation. He said that he understood and was so glad she had shared with him, and that he had accepted Christ! A few weeks later, he died. She was so thankful that God had led her to study, and to memorize, and to be available to her dad. She began to talk with a co-worker who wanted to be discipled. Mary encouraged her to talk to her husband about it, and they started discipling this other couple. (Mary did get her master's degree!)

In short, we have found ourselves developing healthy, enjoyable relationships that last for years! What an exciting and delightful way to spend our lives! Everything we are doing–you can do–and we hope you will!

We are eager to work with people who have a desire to know God, be used by Him in helping others, and who are willing to pay the price of time and effort required. These are people who want to be like Christ. They are willing to die to selfish desires and instead want to be "wholly filled and flooded with God Himself" (Eph. 3:19, AMP). It is a HUGE thing! The Bible says that there are few who get there! (Matt. 7:14) I want to be one of those, don't you? Disciples are careful not to waste their lives and to use their discretionary time wisely. They love and worship God more and more and find themselves loving people–because God does! Great stuff!

ANY OLE BUSH

We firmly believe that any good results are completely due to the grace of God working in their lives. We cannot and do not take any credit. Nor do we get depressed or feel we have failed when folks don't trust the LORD as we hoped. Again, the results are not up to us.

---

[1] A. W. Tozer, *The Knowledge of the Holy*, (Back to the Bible Broadcast, Nebraska, 1961), 7.

Chapter Four
The Holy Spirit–The Fire in the Bush

God has provided only one way to live the Christian life–being controlled by the Holy Spirit. The enabling power of the Holy Spirit allows us to fulfill our ultimate purpose of glorifying God. The Bible expresses the relationship with Christ through the Holy Spirit several different ways. The Scripture uses these specific phrases, "abiding in Christ," "walking in the Spirit," or to be "complete in Christ." To me, the simplest and clearest of all is when Jesus said,

> ...it is the Father, living in me, who is doing his work.
>
> **John 14:10**

Very few people experience that kind of relationship today.

Mind Set

How are we to think of "walking in the Spirit?" It is a *mind set*, a thought process, a way of thinking correctly about God's plan, a matter of the will, and of attitude. This *mind set* results in the freedom for God to give us what we need, such as:

Love for God and people	Obedience
The ability to truly know God	Unselfishness
Humility (and loss of pride)	Guidance of the Holy Spirit
The ability to glorify God	Fruit of the Spirit
Submission	

Any Ole Bush

These results normally flow from a mind that is thinking correctly. But you cannot think correctly without accurate knowledge. Thinking correctly, at least thinking biblically, is a matter of knowing Scripture. So first, you must know Scripture. Second, you must believe what you know, that is reckon, count on, consider it to be true, and put your faith in it. Third, you must be submissive and obey the truth of which you have become convinced.

So, feed your mind! Simple. Anyone can do it! Everyone who wants to can WITS. (That stands for walk in the Spirit–remember?)

How do I get this mind set? Not from school, the media, newspaper, magazines, newscasts, TV, locker rooms, the work place, secular books, vacations in Maui, a picnic in the park, bars, skiing, tennis, golf, bowling, Las Vegas, and certainly not from Hollywood!

Where then? There are three places (mentioned earlier).

1. The Bible
2. Great books about the Bible
3. Fellowship with those who spend time in the first two.

Helping *wanters* to understand these things and live under His control is what we call *discipling*. Isn't it wonderful to realize the simplicity and availability of this mindset to everyone! So, what is the problem?

I believe many are ignorant of God's plan. If people do not study the Bible, then they simply do not know how much God has done for us. This is critical knowledge. You need to know in your heart that God is a sovereign, loving, awesome, and personal God who loves you. You need to be convinced that His plans and ways are better than yours. He has already given you eternal life, justified, regenerated, reconciled, adopted, and made you righteous in His sight. The general lack of understanding of all of this reveals the need for discipleship.

The Holy Spirit—The Fire in the Bush

Mr. Yates

I heard Dr. Bill Bright tell the story of a poor sheep farmer in west Texas. Mr. Yates barely made enough money to exist. What little he possessed, he obtained by grazing a few sheep on his land. But one day, an oil crew received his permission to drill a wildcat well. They hit the biggest pool of oil ever discovered up to that time. Mr. Yates became a multi-millionaire overnight. He owned that oil the day he bought the land, but he didn't know it was there. What a vivid illustration of the fact that when you have Christ within you, you are wealthy beyond comprehension—yet often remain ignorant of who He is and what He has done for you.

How should you respond? It is so simple that anyone can understand it. You can sum it all up in two very significant words, *trust* and *obey*. Unfortunately, it usually takes a long time for a believer to grasp what *trust* and *obey* means. *Trust* in God means that you are convinced of His love, power, and wisdom. The result is joyful submission and obedience to Him. Before you can *trust* God, you must get to know Him. The better you know God, the easier it is to *trust* Him. That's why He gave us the Bible, so we might get to know Him in a personal way. Therefore, we need to *pickle* (soak ourselves) in the Bible.

It Is By Faith!

What does that mean? Faith in what? Answer: faith in God's Word. It is as simple as that. "Trust and obey" as the hymn states. Both are needed.

Major W. Ian Thomas's book, *The Saving Life of Christ* has some great insights:

> There is something which makes Christianity more than a religion, more than ethic, and more than the idle dream of the sentimental idealist. It is this something

that makes it relevant to each one of us right now as a contemporary experience. It is the fact that Christ Himself is the very life content of the Christian faith. It is He who makes it "tick" (1 Thess. 5:24). The One who calls you is the One who does that to which He calls you. "For it is God which worketh in you, both to will and to do of His good pleasure" (Phil. 2:13).

The One who calls you to a life of righteousness is the One who, by your consent, ministers to the needs of humanity through you. This is the divine genius that saves a man from the futility of self-effort (not direct quotes). Thus it is possible for you to take every step in the very energy and power of God Himself, totally dependent upon the life of Christ within you.

"Without me, you can do nothing" (John 15:5). How much can Jesus Christ do through you? Everything.[1]

We cannot live the life Christ died to provide for us without the control and enablement of the Holy Spirit. That is His plan. There is no "Plan B." It takes time to grasp this greatest of all truths. So we need to know *Who* the Holy Spirit is, and how to be controlled by Him as we live each day.

The Holy Spirit is God and is the One who convicts unbelievers of sin and the need for the Savior. At the moment a person is born-again, the Holy Spirit permanently indwells him, gives assurance of forgiveness, regeneration, justification, makes him aware of his adoption as a son, and enables him to know and understand the things of God. The Holy Spirit takes the things of God and makes them real to us. He gives us the power to do the will of God on earth, to live holy lives, to bear fruit and to glorify God. He leads, teaches, protects, and He never leaves us! God has given us four commands:

The Holy Spirit–The Fire in the Bush

1. Be Filled With the Spirit

"Keep on being filled" is the literal translation. Not just once, but continually being filled. It is in the passive mode–something I allow, but that God does. I do not fill myself, I receive the filling. What does *filled* mean? Answer: empowered, controlled, under authority or influence of. When a person is "drunk on wine," he is under the influence of wine. Ephesians 5:18 states, "Do not get drunk on wine, which leads to debauchery. Instead, be filled with the Spirit." Just because you have read that Scripture, it does not mean you are filled with the Spirit.

Filling has two origins: the flesh and the Spirit. So, if there is no boldness, no "fruit of the Spirit," no love, no influence–what is controlling me? What happens when I am not filled?

1. There is no power.
2. My behavior does not reflect the fruit of the Spirit.

2. Do Not Grieve the Holy Spirit

And do not grieve the Holy Spirit of God, with whom you were sealed for the day of redemption.

Ephesians 4:30

To grieve means to cause sorrow, pain, anguish, as in the death of a spouse or child. Grief happens in a relationship of intense love. Shock! God allows Himself to grieve because of me–my disobedience, rebellion, and unfaithfulness. Who is grieved? The Holy Spirit! Since He never leaves, it means that He cannot get away (from my unbelief). When someone hurts you, the one thing you want to do is get away from them. But the Holy Spirit stays. He wants to be close to you because He loves you deeply.

In Acts 5:3, Ananias and his wife lied to the Holy Spirit. What causes a person the most grief? Deep grief comes when an adulterous spouse, or a son who lives in rebellion, turns his/her back on you. Yet, this is exactly what you and I have done to the Holy Spirit! We have willfully sinned, been unfaithful, committed spiritual adultery. What does God do when this happens? He waits, and loves, and chastens.

The average Christian carries a huge load of sin and rebellion, and thus rarely, if ever, is filled with the Spirit. Then he wonders what is wrong and wonders why the Holy Spirit does not speak, lead, or teach him. The solution is to ask the Lord what is grieving Him and fix it. Make a list, perhaps right now, of known sin, then deal with it. Confess your sin first. Then change your mind and your thinking about God's love and grace.

3. Do Not Quench the Holy Spirit

The Holy Spirit is quenched by disobeying a known command, by saying *no* to Him. Do not resist Him. (It is different than grieving, where essentially you say *yes* to sin.) To quench is to "put out the fire." 1 Thessalonians 5:19, (AMP) says, "Do not [quench, subdue] put out the Spirit's fire." To quench is personal resistance to something that God wants you to do. It is when your will conflicts with His will. Submission is needed to deal with the resistance. To submit means that I don't want to, but I choose to do so. *Not wanting to* is not a sin. How you handle it though, may be sin. Your child does not have to want to submit to or agree with you. He only needs to obey. Humans rarely want to submit, but the goal of the Holy Spirit is complete submission, that is, brokenness of our will to His–submission in everything.

What can quench the Holy Spirit?

PEOPLE: We must never let anyone take precedence over God.

"If anyone comes to me and does not hate his father and mother, his wife and children, his brothers and sisters–yes, even his own life–he cannot be my disciple."
Luke 14:26

The Holy Spirit–The Fire in the Bush

POSSESSIONS: Hold everything with an open hand.

"In the same way, any of you who does not give up everything he has cannot be my disciple."

Luke 14:33

Is that too severe? How about:

Jesus answered, "If you want to be perfect, go, sell your possessions and give to the poor, and you will have treasure in heaven. Then come, follow me." When the young man heard this, he went away sad, because he had great wealth.

Matthew 19:21-22

Is there something that you would not give up, if God asked you to?

POWER: Wanting to rule. It is not wrong to want to be great, to be a leader. But in God's plan, greatness lies in servanthood.

"Not so with you. Instead, whoever wants to become great among you must be your servant, and whoever wants to be first must be your slave–just as the Son of Man did not come to be served, but to serve, and to give his life as a ransom for many."

Matthew 20:26-28

Have you ever said *no* when God called you to be a servant?

PLEASURE: Desiring the flesh instead of the Spirit.

A fool finds pleasure in evil conduct, but a man of understanding delights in wisdom.

Proverbs 10:23

He who loves pleasure will become poor; whoever loves wine and oil will never be rich.

Proverbs 21:17

...treacherous, rash, conceited, lovers of pleasure rather than lovers of God...

2 Timothy 3:4

There is nothing wrong with pleasure–of the right sort!

You have made known to me the path of life; you will fill me with joy in your presence, with eternal pleasures at your right hand.

Psalm 16:11

But selfish pleasure-seeking is bad news. Instead, the Bible clearly points us to:

Then Jesus said to his disciples, "If anyone would come after me, he must deny himself and take up his cross and follow me."

Matthew 16:24

"I tell you the truth, unless a kernel of wheat falls to the ground and dies, it remains only a single seed. But if it dies, it produces many seeds. The man who loves his life will lose it, while the man who hates his life in this world will keep it for eternal life."

John 12:24-25

We must believe that we are dead to self.

PLACE: If God calls you to move to Russia, to Montana, to Vietnam–what will you say? If you are not willing–you cannot be filled with the Spirit. Our real citizenship is in heaven. How about Abraham–he lived in tents all his life!

By faith he made his home in the promised land like a stranger in a foreign country; he lived in tents, as did Isaac and Jacob, who were heirs with him of the same promise. For he was looking forward to the city with foundations, whose architect and builder is God.

Hebrews 11:9-10

The Holy Spirit—The Fire in the Bush

Would you be content with a goatskin tent all your life?

FEAR: Instead of trusting God in all circumstances, fear of people, failure, and embarrassment cause us to quench the Spirit in our daily walk.

> *There is no fear in love. But perfect love drives out fear, because fear has to do with punishment. The one who fears is not made perfect in love.*
>
> **1 John 4:18**

> *For you did not receive a spirit that makes you a slave again to fear, but you received the Spirit of sonship. And by him we cry, "Abba, Father."*
>
> **Romans 8:15**

When filled with the Spirit, fear is replaced with boldness.

UNBELIEF: Probably our greatest problem! The root of unbelief is the fact that we do not know God, and thus do not consider Him trustworthy. Unbelief is an overwhelming deterrent, an effective blockade to the Spirit's working in our lives.

4. Walk in the Spirit

Walk is a command, a present imperative. *Keep on walking* in the original Greek language. The focus is not on me (to try my best), but is on the Holy Spirit and His strength. The Holy Spirit and His power is present, but most believers do not walk in the Spirit and rarely even think of the Spirit. *Walk* means habitual conduct, the way you live. If you walk in the Spirit, you will not, will not (emphatic!) sin. The flesh is always there and always seeking to push you into sin. You are dead to it, but sin is not dead! It never goes away! It is not that you have to always fight sin; it is that if you walk in the Spirit, you will not sin. The only victory over the flesh is to walk in the Spirit. There is no *Plan B*.

Any Ole Bush

So I say, live by the Spirit, and you will not gratify the desires of the sinful nature.

Galatians 5:16

You either walk in the Spirit or you walk after the flesh. Walking after the flesh is known as carnal, fleshly, unspiritual, outside the buoys, or doing the best you can. The flesh will never be converted, never get better, and is totally condemned by God. Even after walking with God for sixty years or more, it (the flesh) is still the same.

Those controlled by the sinful nature cannot please God.

Romans 8:8

Let's say that you know the best basketball coach in the world and you want to play on his team. What would you do? You would voluntarily put yourself under his authoritative control. You would do what he said and you would do it *when* he said to do it. That is exactly what it means to *be controlled by the Spirit* or to *walk* in the Spirit. If you choose, you can refuse to do what the coach says. What happens then? You do not get to play on his team until you repent. If you want to enjoy the game, you submit to whatever the coach asks of you. Yielding your will to his, you trust his game plan instead of your own. Everyone understands that!

Normalcy

In Scripture, there are many references to *walk*. It is normal to walk. We are to walk in all His ways, walk blameless, walk in truth, walk uprightly, walk in the light, walk in obedience to His commands, walk in love, and walk in the Spirit. It's so simple! It is a matter of faith. It is God doing it in me, by my consent and obedience. Struggles do not stop when we are filled with the Spirit–it is in the midst of struggles and trials that victory occurs. It is exhilarating and wonderful, a fruitful and joyful way to live. It's available.

The Holy Spirit–The Fire in the Bush

Tozer correctly says, "Every man is as full of the Holy Spirit as he wants to be!"[2]

If I try to live the Christian life by my own effort and determination, it becomes complex, utterly impossible. But if I invite the Lord Jesus to be my life, and if I walk in the light as God is in the light–then the Holy Spirit simply lives His abundant life in me, in all His resurrection power!!!

If you have not yet read Major W. Ian Thomas's book, *The Saving Life of Christ*, this would be a great time to do it. He makes these issues come alive. Another great book on this subject is Watchman Nee's *Sit, Walk, Stand*. My latest and current favorite is Dan Stone's, *The Rest of The Gospel*.

It is all by faith. All of Christian living is by faith in an Almighty God who cannot lie. It is not complicated or beyond our reach. God expects us to simply believe what He says, and act on it.

---

[1] Major W. Ian Thomas, *The Saving Life of Christ*, (Grand Rapids, Michigan, Zondervan, 1961), 13, 15-16.
[2] A. W. Tozer, *The Best of Tozer*, (Grand Rapids, Michigan, Baker Book House Company), 37.

Any Ole Bush

Chapter Five
Spirit-Controlled Helps

How does this marvelous process of discipleship happen? We believe that this is a process which must be relational and personal. That is why it cannot be done in large groups. This book is our attempt to explain how we have discipled many people over the past fifty years and it is our hearts' intent that you will be motivated to become a discerning disciple maker. The Word of God is the solid rock of all our knowledge and belief so that is the place to start. The Phillips translation of 2 Timothy 3:16 says,

> *All scripture is inspired by God and is useful for teaching the faith and correcting error, for re-setting the direction of a man's life and training him in good living. The scriptures are the comprehensive equipment of the man of God and fit him fully for all branches of his work.*

Notice the key words: equipment, re-setting, training (motivate), fit, and work. This verse makes it very clear that knowing the Bible is an absolute necessity.

Tom and Sue

God seeks and uses ordinary people (ordinary bushes), who simply have discovered that He is all they need for life and godliness. People "whose hearts are fully committed to him" (2 Chron. 16:9) are the ones He uses in His work of making disciples.

We had been meeting with Tom and Sue for about two years. They were a great encouragement to us. Having grown very rapid-

Any Ole Bush

ly in their relationship with Christ, they were helping others as well. Tom came from a legalistic church experience, but was very open to God's Word and to spiritual insights. He was a thinker. He read, pondered over Scripture, and prayed. His summary of what it means to walk in the Spirit is worth quoting, especially in view of the fact that he had been digging in biblical truth for such a short time.

> Man's part is to receive the salvation God offers him in Christ. The "dead" man is saved by the grace of God, by the work God does for him, not by anything he does. We have been justified by God's grace. This seems like the first major hill in the contest of walking in the Spirit. For me, this happened as a result of trying to please God by keeping the law. I came to my wits' end when I realized that I could never keep the law, nor could I please God by myself. The answer was for me to trust God. Abiding in Christ means to completely depend on Him to express His life through me. Grace is a system of living whereby God blesses us because we are in Christ and for no other reason at all. Yet many Christians are miserable because they still live with an Old Testament perspective that causes them to try to stay in God's favor by what they do and don't do.
>
> When I began submitting myself to God I really began to see the fruit of walking in the Spirit. It has resulted in a wonderful inner peace, understanding, contentment, a solid peaceful marriage, a desire to help others, love for God, and the assurance of continuing acceptance by God–in short everything that really matters!

You, like Tom, can have the same!

Spirit-Controlled Helps

Characteristics of Spirit-Controlled People

- Eager to study the Bible
- They memorize Scripture
- They have a daily quiet time (an encounter with God)
- They are obedient to God in every area of life
- They seek and enjoy Christian fellowship
- There is a conscious denying of self
- They trust God in everything
- They habitually bring "every thought captive to Christ"
- Humility is a prominent character quality

Is this you? Good! If not–you can fix it!

Wisdom from Spirit-Controlled People

Without being filled with the Spirit, it is impossible for an individual Christian or a church to ever have or work as God desires.[1]

Andrew Murray

The church must be filled with the Spirit. This is the only thing that will help her in the conflict with sin and the world.[2]

Andrew Murray

Without the Spirit of God we can do nothing. We are ships without wind or chariots without steeds. Like branches without sap, we are withered. Like coals without fire–we are useless.[3]

Charles H. Spurgeon

If we look alone to ministers, if we look alone to Christ's disciples to do this work, we shall be disappointed. If we look to the Spirit of God and expect it to come from Him and Him alone, then we shall honor the Spirit and the Spirit will do His work.[4]

D. L. Moody

Any Ole Bush

Understanding the Holy Spirit is the crucial task for Christian Theology at all times. For where the Spirit's Ministry is studied, it will also be sought after. And where it is sought after, spiritual vitality will result.[5]

J.I. Packer, *Keep In Step With The Spirit*

We study and discuss God, Christ, the church, mission, Christian social involvement, and many other things; we pay lip service to the Holy Spirit throughout (everyone does these days) but we are not yet taking Him seriously in any of it. In this, we need to change.

Unknown

The Struggle of Carnal People

The Bible says that you are dead to sin, you are complete in Christ, God has given you everything you need for life and godliness, you have Christ Himself living in your heart, you are indwelt by the Holy Spirit, and you have access to the mind of the living Christ.

We have noticed over many years of discipling people that many are still struggling with pride, selfishness, lust, anger, and deceit. Why is this? Galatians 5:16 says, "So I say, live by the Spirit, and you will not gratify the desires of the sinful nature." Do you believe that? And how about this passage, "But we have this treasure in jars of clay to show that this all-surpassing power is from God and not from us" (2 Cor. 4:7).

A young wife (a strong believer) called one day, heartbroken. Her Christian husband was going to spend some *happy hour* time at a local bar with his co-workers (including some women) instead of coming home for dinner. He had done so once before and had come home drunk. She wanted to know how to respond. Jan advised her to ask God for wisdom, to trust Him for the outcome, to pray for her husband, not to nag him about this matter, and to apologize for getting on his back about it earlier. (Thankfully, it turned out well.)

Spirit-Controlled Helps

This is not unusual today, but it should be. What are believers thinking when they choose to spend time hanging out at a bar with co-workers instead of being home with the kids and wife?

Like learning to drive a car, a lot of basic information is needed, which we acquire over time by consistent Bible study, prayer, and fellowship. Like driving, once learned, it is easy, and automatic. Basics like humility, obedience, prayer, verse by verse study, and memorization become spiritually natural. We think the 1-ON-1, explained in Chapter Three, is an excellent guide to these truths.

Two Anchors

Early in our Christian walk we dropped a couple of anchors (major convictions).

1. The Bible is the Word of God. We totally depend on it for our thinking, teaching, and living.
2. God will live His life through us. In fact, He *IS* our life.

All we need to do is to be available to Him by faith.

It took some time before I realized in a very practical way how to be available. The 1-ON-1 workbook we use as our game plan is enormously helpful to this end. We, like many others, did not understand the work of the Holy Spirit. Being utterly self-centered, I had no interest in people. So it is not me, it is God, by His grace, and through the enablement of His Holy Spirit, that I can love people. He motivated me to spend my life seeking to help others.

Life is short. Someone suggested it is represented simply by the dash between two dates, e.g. 1924-2008. That little dash is all we have! So, we wanted our time on earth to matter, to make a difference. We wanted to honor God and to raise godly kids.

Knowing our purpose was of tremendous value in making decisions like how to spend our time, money, and energy. So, one of our top priorities was to *be there* for our family. It paid off. Both of our children are strong in the Lord. They have happy, fruitful marriages, their kids are headed in the right direction, and they are good examples for others.

Jan recalls this situation:

> When our kids were young, we were very involved with *Young Life* and *Campus Crusade for Christ*. I was eager to spend more and more time and energy with these ministries. I remember struggling with this decision. During our children's teen years, I was so concerned about all the people who needed to hear the gospel that I pushed for us to be more involved in those meetings. But Bert always emphasized our need to spend time with the kids and was very careful not to short change the family for the ministry. I am so grateful for his heart to keep that focus. Balance is the key word here.

We happily trusted the Lord to give us balance and wisdom. Actually, we ask for and expect to get, His wisdom in every area, every day. We counted on it for raising the kids, time management decisions, career matters, spiritual discernment, where to live, who to talk to, and what to say–in short, everything!

We are so thankful for that mindset over the years. After our daughter was grown, she shared an example of how time with the children paid off. When our daughter was sixteen, we were out of town teaching in a conference. Jan's parents were baby sitting. Two boys in the senior class at our daughter's high school (she was dating one of them at the time) invited her to go with them to California. Her plan was to crawl out her bedroom window late at night after the grandparents thought she had gone to bed, and to go with them! Many years later she told us that the only reason she did not go was that she had such great respect for her dad. She knew this would really hurt him. So, she did not go!

Spirit-Controlled Helps

What incredible things God does for our protection, and we are totally unaware of it! (I cannot tell, or even write that story without getting choked up.)

Expectations

We have come to expect great things because our confidence is not in ourselves, but in God. We know we can depend on God's presence and power to use us as a channel of blessing and life-change to others. Our source is the Sovereign God of the universe, the Holy Spirit living within our spirit, and by our permission, living His life in us. You can't do better than that!

It took a while for me to understand that God's only plan for living the Christian life (and for influencing others) was for me to be controlled by the Holy Spirit. I needed to own the truth that I could not live the life, or cause spiritual growth in others, by study and effort. Several things helped me come (gradually) to the conscious awareness of how to do it.

I was sitting in my car one day talking to a friend who asked if I had totally committed my whole life to Christ. I said, "Oh sure, I think I have. It certainly is my desire." So, he suggested I make sure in my own mind by praying right there in the car. I told God that I wanted to drive down a stake and make sure I was totally His. Romans 12:1 says, "in view of God's mercy" make a decisive dedication of your whole life to Him. I did that in the car that day.

Bill Bright's teaching of the Holy Spirit's place in my daily life was of tremendous help to cement these truths in my thinking. I have shared the *Spirit-Filled Life*[6] booklet with quite a few people over the years. Never forget:

...it is the Father, living in me, who is doing his work.

John 14:10

When understood, that single phrase says it all!

ANY OLE BUSH

[1] Andrew Murray, *Experiencing the Holy Spirit*, (New Kensington, Pennsylvania, Whitaker House, 1984), 7.
[2] Ibid., 29.
[3] *52 QUOTES* Compiled By: Dr. Paul Chappell, Pastor of Lancaster Baptist Church, 4020 E. Lancaster Blvd., Lancaster, CA.
[4] D.L. Moody, *Secret Power*, (New Kensington, Pennsylvannia, Whitaker House, 1991), 8.
[5] J. I. Packer, *Keep In Step With The Spirit*, (Grand Rapids, Michigan, Fleming Revell, 1987), 236.
[6] Available at www.cci.org

Chapter Six
Obedience–How Much is Enough?

Obedience is something without which you cannot do.

Paul said in 2 Corinthians 2:9, "The reason I wrote you was to see if you would stand the test and be obedient in everything." Jesus said in Luke 6:46, "Why do you call me, 'Lord, Lord,' and do not do what I say?"

A. W. Tozer said, "The most important thing about anyone, is what they think–when they think about God. To think of God as less than, or other than He is, is idolatry."[1]

This all drives me to realize that obedience has vast importance. If I perceive God to be as He is, then anything other than implicit obedience is insanity. Yet, very few of us are seriously concerned about disobedience. Obedience is the opposite of having my own way. As stated earlier, a national law-enforcement conference determined that the biggest fundamental problem in the world is the lack of respect for authority. Webster's dictionary states that obedience is to "comply with a known command, law or duty." Obedience then, is "proper submission to authority." It has to be learned. Hebrews 5:8 says Jesus, "learned obedience from what he suffered."

A class of 250 college students was told that a paper was due at the end of September, October, and November. Failure to hand in the paper by the 30th of the month was an automatic *F*. Everyone understood the rules, but only 225 turned in papers on September 30th.

ANY OLE BUSH

However, after much crying and begging, the professor gave the 25 late ones another chance. At the end of the next month, there were 50 late papers. Again, the professor extended mercy to them–giving them more time to complete the assignment. The certainty of failure, should the last deadline be missed, was again clearly stated by the professor. Sure enough, at the end of the third month, 100 students were late. All were give an *F* (failure) for the course. "Unfair," they all complained.

They had taken mercy (suspension of justice) for granted. They presumed on the professor's patience. Obedience was not important to them. These students experienced two doses of mercy in only two months. God has been showing mercy to all of us for thousands of years in countless situations. Do we think His justice will never come? Are we taking His mercy and patience for granted?

Do we think God is careless about obedience to Him? Does it make any difference (really!) if we are disobedient? Although we readily perceive God as loving, kind, incredibly patient, and merciful, we need to also realize that God is the Sovereign Creator, that He is absolutely holy, just, and fair. He knows everything, is everywhere, and never lies or exaggerates. He hates sin. Disobedience to the Creator God is the height of foolishness. Generally, how are you doing as far as obedience goes? Pretty good? Not too bad?

I did some serious thinking about my own obedience a few years ago. I want you to think about it right now! Take time to honestly consider how you are doing in these areas:

STUDY: "Do your best to present yourself to God as one approved...who correctly handles the word of truth" (2 Tim. 2:15).

THANKSGIVING: "give thanks in all circumstances." (1 Thess. 5:18).

PRAYER: "Pray continually;" (1Thess. 5:17) about everything, day and night, pray for one another, when you pray believe, devote

Obedience–How Much is Enough?

yourself to prayer, pray for those who persecute you, and do not use meaningless repetition.

LUST: Most people are guilty here. Are you? "But I tell you that anyone who looks at a woman lustfully has already committed adultery with her in his heart" (Matt. 5:28).

THOUGHT LIFE: "...take captive every thought to make it obedient to Christ" (2 Cor. 10:5). Are your words and thoughts acceptable to God?

LOVE: Love for God–Do you love God with all your heart all the time? (Of course not, no one does!) Is it important that you keep this, the greatest of all the commandments? Is that a concern for you? (I basically ignored it for years.) Love for my spouse–"just as Christ loved the church and gave himself up for her" (Eph. 5:25). How are you doing with this one?

SUBMISSION: This is one of the biggest demands for the Christian. Jesus is our transcendent example. Husbands and wives, this is your calling from God toward your spouse. "Submit to one another out of reverence for Christ" (Eph. 5:21). All of us are to submit to one another. It's almost a non-entity in our world today, isn't it? How do you feel about this?

LOVE FOR PEOPLE: Christians are part of our spiritual family. "This is my command: Love each other" (John 15:17). Do you?

RESPONSE TO ADVERSITY: This is another *biggie*. How do you respond to an unreasonable boss, or spouse, or situation? 1 Peter 3:1 says our response should be "they may be won over without words by the behavior..."–no vengeance. Is that the way you handle it? James 1:2 says to "consider it pure joy, my brothers, whenever you face trials of many kinds." Do you?

Is it reasonable to walk through a day being constantly disobedient to God in these and other areas, and yet expect to enjoy God's blessings and control of His Holy Spirit? I don't think so!

Lessons Learned

I had a chance to put a lot of this good stuff into practice not too long ago. I underwent an artificial hip replacement. It was without doubt the most miserable, pain-filled experience of my life. I also found that God was adequate to meet my needs, and did. I experienced the reality of peace and joy in the midst of physical pain.

Obeying rules can be critical to life. As an anesthesiologist, I always insisted that my patients, who were to have surgery the next morning, not eat or drink anything at all for twelve hours prior to their surgery. Why? To avoid the serious risk of death from regurgitation of stomach contents while unconscious. God strongly insists that we obey Him. Why? He knows that if we follow His instructions, we will be safe. He has our best interests at heart. If we submit to His Will, we will experience His resources.

As we obey God, we begin to understand more of who He is. Why? Obedience is intimately associated with worship. Worship is a result of an obedient heart.

Yet a time is coming and has now come when the true worshipers will worship the Father in spirit and truth, for they are the kind of worshipers the Father seeks. God is spirit, and his worshipers must worship in spirit and in truth.

John 4:23-24

How can I know the truth about God? The answer:

Whoever has my commands and obeys them, he is the one who loves me. He who loves me will be loved by my Father, and I too will love him and [will make myself real to him] show myself to him.

John 14:21

Obedience–How Much is Enough?

Think about it! Obedience is the only door into the place where God reveals Himself! If that is true (and it is), then obedience assumes incredible importance. Worship and obedience are more than related, they are almost synonymous! Have you ever found it difficult to worship God? I have. I wonder if daily, repeated, thoughtless, disobedience has anything to do with that? What do you think?

In the Old Testament, Saul tried *partial obedience.* He tried to pull the wool over God's eyes and obeyed partially, but God didn't buy it. It is spelled out in 1 Samuel 15. Partial obedience is disobedience.

Does the thought of partial obedience make you feel uncomfortable? It is my conviction that most of us do not believe that thought is worth a lot of fuss. We believe that God will only deal with us in love and grace, and that His mercy will insulate us from His justice. We know He is longsuffering, but God's mercy does have an end-point! The Bible says sin carries enormous consequences! To presume on God's mercy and grace is foolish–maybe stupid is a better word!

What is your motive for obeying God? Is it:
- To gain acceptance with God?
- To get what you want from Him?
- Fear of severe punishment if you don't?
- Or is it from your deep love for God?

> If you know Him,
> You'll love Him.
> If you love Him,
> You will serve Him.
> If you don't serve Him,
> You don't love Him.
> And if you don't love Him,
> You don't know Him.

Deny Self

The greatest hindrance to *WITS* (walking in the Spirit) is the reluctance to deny self. The very essence of human sin is bound up in wanting your own way. "We all, like sheep, have gone astray, each of us has turned to his own way; and the LORD has laid on him the iniquity of us all" (Isa. 53:6). To deny yourself of what your nature most desires is huge. You may work, study, do good deeds, go to church, memorize verses, give money, go on mission trips, and the like, but the one thing you may not do is to deny self. Selfishness is an unwillingness to exchange your will for His will. Yet that is the anchor of true Christianity. That is exactly what Jesus did when He came to the earth. Jesus said,

> *...because I do not seek or consult My own will [I have no desire to do what is pleasing to Myself, My own aim, My own purpose] but only the will and pleasure of the Father Who sent Me.*
>
> **John 5:30, AMP**

What a tremendous statement!

In Romans 12:1, Paul urges a decisive dedication of all that you are and will be, to God. To do this utterly blocks the idea of two masters. Instead, you die to self, and live to Christ. Romans 6:11 says, "In the same way, count yourselves dead to sin but alive to God in Christ Jesus."

What does dying to self look like? It is the opposite of being alive to self. This kind of life allows you to live in complete victory. Measure your life with the following that was used of God in bringing revival during the Boston Awakening of 1909.

Obedience–How Much is Enough?

Victory[1]

When you are forgotten, or neglected, or purposely set at naught, and you smile inwardly, glorying in the insult or the oversight–That is Victory!

(John 13:26-30; 2 Tim. 4:16-18)

When your good is evil spoken of, when your wishes are crossed, your taste offended, your advice disregarded, your opinions ridiculed, and you take it all in patient and loving silence–That is Victory!

(John 8:48-50; 2 Tim. 4:16-18; 2 Peter 2:20-21)

When you can bear with any discord, any irregularity and unpunctuality, any annoyance–and are content with any food, any raiment, any climate, any society, any solitude, any interruption–That is Victory!

(Phil 4:11-13; Heb. 11:3-11; Acts 27:21-25; 2 Cor. 4:8-10)

When you never care to refer to yourself in conversation or to record your own good works, or to itch after commendation, when you can truly "love to be unknown"–That is Victory!

(Gal. 2:20; 6:14)

Humility

Dying to selfish ambition, and relying on God as your source of ambition requires humility. Humility is a rare quality today, but an absolute necessity if you want to live as God intends. Andrew Murray says that humility is,

> *"...the place of entire dependence upon God, is from the very nature of things the first duty and the highest virtue of His creatures. It is not something that we bring to God, or that He bestows; it is simply the sense of entire nothingness that comes when we see how truly God is everything."*[2]

ANY OLE BUSH

It is vital to *WITS*! You will never see people walking in the Spirit unless this is their mind set too. Consider these thoughts from Andrew Murray's book *Humility: The Journey Toward Holiness*. This is a book we all need to read repeatedly. It needs to become a vital part of our thinking.

Humility is total and entire dependence on God. It is from the very nature of things, the first duty and highest virtue of man (see quote from page 16 above), the chief mark of every Christian. "And so pride–the loss of humility–is the root of every sin and evil."[3]

> *Without this [humility] there can be no true abiding in God's presence or experience of His favor and the power of His Spirit; without this no abiding faith or love or joy or strength. Humility is the only soil in which virtue takes root; a lack of humility is the explanation of every defect and failure.*[4]

The lack of it is sufficient explanation of man's every defect and failure and the source of all the wretchedness of our world! It is pride that made redemption necessary; it is from our pride that we need, above everything else, to be redeemed.[5] Our only hope is the life of Christ within us.

Murray's statements concerning humility are quite challenging. Notice these:

> *It is the first and chief mark of the relationship of the creature to God, of the Son to the Father–it is the secret of blessedness, the desire to be nothing, that allows God to be all in all.*[6]

> *We may find professors and ministers, evangelists and Christian workers, missionaries and teachers, in whom the gifts of the Spirit are many and manifest, and who are the channels of blessing to multitudes, but of whom, when tested, or close interpersonal relationships reveal their true characters, it is only too evident that the grace of humility, as an abiding characteristic, is rarely to be seen.*[7]

Obedience–How Much is Enough?

Second, is the reality that external teaching and personal effort are powerless to conquer pride or create the meek and lowly heart in a person.[8]

Humility toward men is the only evidence that our humility before God is real! (See 1 John 4:20) The one who has seen himself to be nothing, having died to self, no longer needs to compare himself with others. He feels no jealousy or envy; he can praise God when others are preferred (or promoted) before him. He is not impatient, touchy, or grouchy.

The lack of holiness and humility reveals itself not only in words or thoughts, but in a tone of voice, a way of speaking to others which betrays our selfishness.

It is easy to think that we humble ourselves before God, but our humility toward others is the only sufficient proof that our humility before God is real.[9]

True humility comes when before God we see ourselves as nothing, have put aside self, and let God be all. The soul that has done this, and can say, 'I have lost myself in finding you,' no longer compares itself with others.[10]

The humble person feels no jealousy or envy. He can praise God when others are preferred and blessed before him.[11]

The chief mark of counterfeit holiness is its lack of humility.[12]

And according to what we have of God will be our real humility, because humility is nothing but the disappearance of self in the vision that God is all.[13]

It [the pride of holiness] is a tone, a way of speaking of oneself or others, in which those who have the gift of discernment cannot but recognize the power of self.[14]

"Humility is often identified with penitence and contrition. As a consequence, there appears to be no way of fostering humility but by keeping the soul occupied with its sin."[15] "We have seen in the teaching of our LORD Jesus and the Epistles how often the virtue is mentioned without any reference to sin."[16] The secret of humility is not in the lack of daily sinning, "It [humility] is the displacement of self by the enthronement of God."[17] Strong self-condemnation (which is actually being occupied with self) does not result in humility. According to Murray, "It is not sin, but God's grace showing a man and ever reminding him what a sinner he was that will keep him truly humble."[18] Grace alone causes humility to work as your nature. Don't be occupied with your sin, be occupied with God!

You can have very strong intellectual conviction and still hold pride in your heart! Pride renders faith (and humility) impossible. No wonder our faith is so weak when pride still reigns in our heart![19]

It is a mistake to work diligently to increase your faith without victory over selfishness and pride. You need first of all to humble yourself under the mighty hand of God and gladly accept whatever works to humble you before Him. Then, content to be nothing, you will grow strong in faith, giving glory to God. So, accept what your fellow man does to try or vex you as a means of grace to humble you.

> *That is why, for Christ's sake, I delight in weaknesses, in insults, in hardships, in persecutions, in difficulties. For when I am weak, then I am strong.*
>
> **2 Corinthians 12:10**

"Claim in faith the death and the life of Jesus as your own."[20] "Yes, let us ask whether we have learned to regard a reproof, just or unjust, a reproach from a friend or an enemy, an injury, or trouble, or difficulty as an opportunity for proving that Jesus is all to us."[21]

Obedience–How Much is Enough?

God said, "For everyone who exalts himself will be humbled, and he who humbles himself will be exalted." (Luke 18:14).

Romans 12:1

One of the reasons an eagle stays in the chicken yard is that he is ignorant of who he is, and the extent of his marvelous potential. He may even think he wants to live the rest of his life in the chicken yard. He is there by his own choice. He needs only to spread his wings and let the wind lift him into the sky. He already possesses the equipment he needs.

You have the risen sovereign Christ living in your heart. You cannot have more, and you need not have less. If you are an eagle and are tired of luke-warm, chicken style living, this is going to be an exciting eye-opener for you!

Concentrate for a few minutes on this:

> *I APPEAL to you therefore, brethren, and beg of you in view of [all] the mercies of God, to make a decisive dedication of your bodies [presenting all your members and faculties] as a living sacrifice, holy (devoted, consecrated) and well pleasing to God, which is your reasonable (rational, intelligent) service and spiritual worship.*
>
> **Romans 12:1** AMP

Romans 12:1 is a "drive-a-stake" type specific event. It is not the end, but the beginning of *WITS*. The next verse, Romans 12:2 goes on to tell us we need a daily, on going mental transformation, a renewal of the mind, an on going, daily, continuous thing accomplished by daily time with God in prayer and Bible study. It is something I do and enjoy thoroughly. It is not the onerous duty it once was. As I soak in God's Word and enjoy Him, I find myself wanting to "bring every thought captive to Christ" which is a necessary part of living the Christian life. Since the sin that so easily upsets us starts in the mind, you need to "take it captive." In practical terms, that means when I have a selfish, lustful, or nasty thought, I simply say, "Lord, I don't want to think that way. I want to exchange that thought for the things that honor You and please You and give You glory." And poof–the nasty thought is gone. It never need sit in my mind for more than a few seconds. Simple, but not always easy.

It is natural for a person who has made a decisive dedication of his body to want to please God. It does not require constant supervision. Since you are spiritually being who you really are, you naturally do the right thing. It is unnatural to live selfishly, because you are acting according to who you used to be, but are not now. Breathing is something you do naturally. You don't have to supervise it or even think about it. We immediately respond to anything that hinders natural breathing because not breathing is unnatural. In the real world, when one doesn't breathe, he turns blue. Blue is not a good thing! In medicine, it is called *cyanosis* and requires something to be done immediately!

Bill Bright coined the phrase *spiritual breathing* to help folks understand how it works in the real everyday world. We exhale the impurities (carbon dioxide), and also take in a fresh load of oxygen by inhaling. When you sin, you exhale by confession of that sin (1 John 1:9) and then, by faith, inhale by once again putting yourself under the control of the Holy Spirit. Thus, it only takes a few seconds to maintain your walk in the Spirit.

Real World? (Mike)

How does this work in the real world? I had been meeting with Mike for a few years watching God work in his life. Mike had taken off from the chicken yard and was fast becoming a "faithful man" (a productive bush) who was able to teach others. He told me that I was the first Christian person ever to take a personal interest in him. No one before had asked him about his walk with God, time spent in the Bible, or his hang-ups. "You spent time with me, and were

Obedience–How Much is Enough?

available to meet with me. You listened to my rambling, and challenged me to spend time getting to know and love God." He was hiking in the bottom of the Grand Canyon one day, thinking about purpose, and happened to read 1 Thessalonians 5:24, "And we urge you, brothers, warn those who are idle, encourage the timid, help the weak, be patient with everyone." Mike said God used that verse to cause him to believe that God was personal and real, and it was then and there that he accepted Christ as his personal Savior.

Later I asked Mike, "How do you teach someone to walk in the Spirit?" This was his answer:

> The first thing laid before me was the question, "What is your purpose?" After sorting through the variety of interests I had formed, I realized that they were nothing more than objectives. They were not unified in a single purpose. I perceived it the way the world does–arriving at a purpose after completion of many activities. Purpose must precede and be the pool from which spring the objectives we set for ourselves. For example, we do not start to train for the rigors of a marathon without the purpose of entering and winning. Ephesians 5:15 says "live purposefully" and this was a foreign idea to me. To look upon one's life and evaluate it as objectively as possible is NOT encouraged in the world. The world had kept me dulled by its stimulants of pop culture and gratification so that I did not consider a real purpose of my life. Arriving at my purpose, (to please God) laid the foundation for the next question, "How?"
>
> Bert gave me *The Spiritual Life* by Andrew Murray and looking back through my journal, it was during this time that I experienced the glorious breakthrough that Romans 5:8 promises. I had never understood the division between a carnal and Spirit-filled Christian. It was

through great books like this that God began to reform my thinking. After years of putting the world's thinking in my "vat," God used these books to reveal that His depth was something worth diving into. I devoured them.

At the same time, God was using Bert's personal walk to light a burning in my own heart to know the Word of God. I believe the opportunity to see the passion in another man for God's Word is very rare. It is even rarer for such a person to open his life for inspection; i.e., his marriage, his home, and his dealings with people, and in so doing, silently teach how a godly man lives.

So, I began to experience God's love personally through his patient, gentle guidance. He spent many hours praying for me and my growth. I would rattle off my own personal views and Bert would just nod his head believing that the Lord would soon replace my thinking with His own.

God used this kind of teaching and commitment to change my mind about life. I learned that only Christ's life is a life worth having and the kind of life I was trying to live could only be lived by God. I was released from an ongoing problem of sex and love addiction. The desire for pleasure was replaced by the desire for His pleasure. I had to learn that will power is no power at all unless it is Christ's power. I had to learn that I can't, but He can. I needed to learn that "I have been crucified with Christ; it is no longer I who live, but Christ lives in me; and the life which I now live I live by faith in the Son of God, who loved me and gave Himself for me" (Gal. 2:20).

Obedience–How Much is Enough?

I know that His Holy Spirit lives in me now and I am walking in Him. I have just begun. But, if this glimmer of peace and joy which I have experienced so far are any indication of what it is like to please Him eternally, I look with great expectancy to be used by Him to share His life with others.

Here are some suggestions I made to a young man that I think are worthy: Start the night before by planning to get adequate sleep so you will feel like getting up to spend time in personal fellowship with God. When you wake in the morning, make it your first priority to pray and thank God for the day ahead. Then, quickly review in your mind and in prayer all that God is to you in Christ. Then remember that you are "dead to sin" and alive in Christ and that you can grab by faith all that Holy Spirit has for you. I encourage you to use the *Daily Reminder*, a page of thoughts from God's Word, that I use to help me reset my thinking. You could use mine, or make up your own. Here is what mine looks like.

Daily Reminder

- Lord, You are Sovereign. You know everything. You have infinite wisdom. Your power is limitless. Your timing is always perfect. You are present everywhere and You love me.
- Father, You are worthy of all honor, praise, and worship.
- You designed me for Yourself, to do good works planned before I was born.
- You have always loved me. You chose me before the world began.
- I have been crucified, quickened, raised, and seated with Christ.

- I am dead to sin and I am alive in you!
- I am indwelt by Your Holy Spirit and am complete in Christ.
- I accept the reality of the Holy Spirit's control of my life–right now. Father, You have already provided for everything I will ever need.
- You are enabling me right now to live a holy life that pleases You. I want to turn away from my pride, sin, and selfishness (my focus on myself).
- Instead, I willingly surrender myself completely and cheerfully to You.
- Help me to be more aware of You, to take all my thoughts captive to You and to be obedient to all that I know–to do only Your will.
- Lord, show me where I am disobedient, where I am not pleasing to You.
- Lord, I trust You. I love You. I worship and praise You.
- Now Lord, I thank You in advance for what You have for me today.

How long would that take? Three minutes or so! Then, after breakfast, you could spend some time in quiet reflection on Scripture. The purpose is to sense God's presence (to have an encounter with God) and to set a direction you will be happy with at the end of the day. Romans 8:5 says, "Those who live according to the sinful nature have their minds set on what that nature desires; but those who live in accordance with the Spirit have their minds set on what the Spirit desires."

---

[1] Printed and handed out during Boston's Awakening of 1909 under guidance of Dr. J. Wilbur Chapman: original–source unknown. See note on
http://www.kerryskinner.com/page1/page24/page31/page31.html.

Obedience–How Much is Enough?

[2] Andrew Murray, *Humility: The Journey Toward Holiness*, (Minneapolis, Minnesota, Christian Literature Crusade, 2001), 16-17.
[3] Ibid., 16.
[4] Ibid., 17.
[5] Ibid., 24.
[6] Ibid., 18.
[7] Ibid., 46.
[8] Ibid., 46-47.
[9] Ibid., 53.
[10] Ibid., 55.
[11] Ibid., 55.
[12] Ibid., 61.
[13] Ibid., 63.
[14] Ibid., 65.
[15] Ibid., 69.
[16] Ibid., 69.
[17] Ibid., 69.
[18] Ibid., 72.
[19] Ibid., 73.
[19] Ibid., 77-78.
[20] Ibid., 86.
[21] Ibid., 92.

Any Ole Bush

Chapter Seven
Life Purpose

There is a significant difference between doing things right and doing the right things. How do you "keep the main thing, the main thing!" What is the *main thing*? Without a defined purpose, a person stumbles through life's alleyways in a dense fog not knowing which way to turn, who to follow, or what to do next. A person without purpose is not headed anywhere in particular, so it does not matter which road he takes, where he is, or what he is worth.

That is what I wanted Larry to think about when I asked him, "What are you giving your life to?" Purpose is defined as a "firm intent toward an objective." Activities are used to reach an objective, which has been determined by your purpose. A goal is a sort of waypoint, to help you toward the objective. Most folks have some objectives, and are overloaded with activities, but few have defined a biblical life-purpose. Activities without objectives are frustrating. So are objectives without purpose. It would be very valuable for those who have read this far to take enough time to get your purpose in sharp focus.

A helpful booklet called *Establishing Your Purpose* (published by Vision Foundation Inc. in 1986, but no longer available), states that according to the Bible, God has three levels of purpose:

- *Ultimate* purpose, which includes the whole created order functioning as God intended.

- *Universal* purpose, which is identical for all people–to glorify God and participate in His will. It involves knowing God and being involved with what He is doing.
- *Unique* purpose is specific to every individual. You are is responsible to discover, and be committed to what God has for you. To do so includes understanding how God has gifted you, and what He has equipped and called you to do.

To sort this out and live it, is not a single declaration or event, but a process that takes time. The end product of this process should be a clear, written statement of purpose. Without a clearly defined purpose, activities will be determined by the pressures and demands of the environment rather than the Word of God! What currently determines your activities?

Here are some ideas to help you work through this process. You need to recognize the following:

Spiritual Gifts

Everyone has them. You need to understand your spiritual gifts in order to make wise decisions relating to purpose, and you need to be equipped.

Equipping

This has to do mainly with becoming a man/woman of God, "pickled" (saturated) in Scripture, and filled with the Spirit.

Skills

Skills have to do with what you have learned in life and your areas of competence.

History

History relates to your culture, parents, and background.

Life Purpose

Status

Status deals with your role whether it is husband, wife, parent, or employer, and with physical capabilities and geographical location. Living in America, you will probably have little effect in India.

Temperament

Temperament considers your personality type.

All of these influence the development of your biblical purpose.

> The most important thing to know about anything is its purpose.

You would not try to write with a hammer, or pound a nail with a pencil. I once noticed an airplane sitting on a grass runway, and nearby was a tractor plowing a field. I thought, "that plane is absolutely useless to the farmer; it could not plow a single foot. The tractor could never get me off the ground, but both are effective when used according to their designed purpose."

Take time to think and write down what God is showing you, with the intent of fulfilling God's purpose for you. Determine to do His will instead of your own for the rest of your life. Exciting stuff, isn't it?

> Important activities do not make your life meaningful,
> A meaningful life makes your activities important!

ANY OLE BUSH

You have no guarantee that you will possess the physical, mental, and material resources to achieve your present goals, but with your life purpose intact, you will still be (and feel) significant. Tozer has stated that "the most important thing about you is what you think when you think about God," and "the most important thing about your life is its direction."

Maybe you would like to make this verse your purpose:

that you may be filled [through all your being] [c]unto all the fullness of God [may have the richest measure of the divine Presence, and become a body wholly filled and flooded with God Himself]!

Ephesians 3:19, AMP

Many eagles are still in the chicken yard due to a lack of purpose. Paul said, "[For my determined purpose is] that I may know Him" (Phil. 3:10, AMP). Jesus knew that His purpose was "to do the will of my Father." Purpose determines where you will spend your time, money, and energy. If your goal is to be the world's greatest tennis player, your activities will be entirely different than the person whose goal is to make $100 million by age 35.

God's *universal* purpose for all people is to glorify Him, but there is a *unique* purpose for you and me! You are responsible to discover and commit your life to the purpose that God has for you. Most have never done it, so I always ask about it. To sort this out in your thinking and life is not a single event, but a process that takes time.

As you consider this vital issue, take time to make notes as to what God is teaching you. Your intent is to discover and fulfill God's will for your entire life. Purpose is BIG!

When I was a child, I used to go on house calls with my father, who was a doctor. I intended to be a doctor some day. That was my goal, and I have done so, but it was many years later that I learned

Life Purpose

the importance of a life purpose. When I first thought about it, I decided that my purpose was to please God, although I was not clear on what it was exactly that pleased Him. So, I studied that for a while. Later, after much thought and prayer, I progressed to the idea of knowing God. That is a very deep and wonderful purpose. Lately, I have come to understand that my deepest desire and purpose is to glorify God, and that the only way I can do that is by walking in the Spirit. Jonathan Edwards has written an entire book with the message that the ultimate purpose for all of creation is to bring glory to God.

The Lord said there would always be troubles and trials. Jesus said, "I have told you these things, so that in me you may have peace. In this world you will have trouble. But take heart! I have overcome the world" (John 16:33). The agonies of stress, selfishness, wasted life, impatience, and the like can be greatly accentuated when one knows his purpose.

Any Ole Bush

Chapter Eight
Potholes on the Road to Discipleship

Impatience is a form of unbelief. We all feel it when we doubt the wisdom of God's timing or the wisdom of His guidance. Impatience rises up inside us when our plan is upended. It may be prompted by a long wait in a checkout line, or a sudden, unexpected event. The opposite of impatience is not a glib denial of loss. It is a deepening, peaceful willingness to wait for God and to trust Him with every situation including a solution and its timing. Patience means to walk with God at His pace.

No one "walks in the Spirit" all day every day, although they could, but you can learn to quickly recover from a poor response or a lustful thought. You are just one prayer away from walking in the Spirit, which can take only a few seconds! It is a choice we make many times every day. Just as an eagle can spread his wings and soar anytime he wants to, we can walk in the Spirit when we want to! This is God's plan for every Christian. Is that what you desire? If so, it will cost you having your own way. You will have to exchange your selfishness, pride, lust, unbelief, disobedience, and the like for the life of Christ. A life of peace and love is available to everyone who has the Spirit of Christ (the Holy Spirit) living in them. WHAT A DEAL! What an enormous mistake then for any eagle to putter around in the chicken yard till he looks and smells and thinks like a chicken!

Any Ole Bush

Maybe you would like to drive down a stake (make a decisive dedication) right now and commit all that you are and hope to be to the LORD. Living with the mindset where you are willing to, "offer your bodies as living sacrifices, holy and pleasing to God," (Rom. 12:1), you will find yourself eager to spend time getting to know God better. The purpose of studying the Scripture and memorizing key verses is to meditate and ponder for yourself the things God shows you. Paul said, near the end of his fruitful life, that his desire and purpose was to know God. I have that same goal, and so do many others. We need to encourage each other to this end. Nothing in this world is as valuable as knowing and loving God.

I really want to live with that mind set so I can be a model of the real thing. Craig and I spent considerable time together sharing these great truths with each other. (He is noteworthy because he has raised a godly family of eleven children.) One day, he sent me this note about modeling:

> The most helpful things about our time with you and Jan was that you modeled the walk with the LORD, both personally and in your marriage. You and Jan embodied the walks and marriage my wife and I sought. The LORD was the focal point and the fruit of the Spirit was routinely recognized and demonstrated. Second, your ministry focused on first-hand faith, tailored to meet needs and focused on us as individuals. You were able to encourage others effectively because both you and Jan express what God has done and continues doing. Your prime encouragement was your active, alive, and vital faith. You successfully sowed and watered, and then by God's grace, a great work has been done in our hearts. Third, you listened well, and never answered with what I wanted to hear, but with truth. That is why others trust you and seek out your ministry.

Potholes on the Road to Discipleship

As you can imagine, that note was a very special personal encouragement to me.

Distractions

A common reason for lack of a close walk with God is distractions. You have to learn to deal with them or you will never get to know God. The list of successful distractions seems to be endless. Distractions come from every direction to annoy you. Work, radio, family, TV, phone calls, yard work, plumbing problems, financial pressures, lousy relationships, bad news, unpleasant neighbors, loud music, bad weather, relatives, machines that don't work, and computers that crash are just a few of life's distractions. Can a person realistically be expected to WITS in today's environment? Absolutely–and thrive! We are "more than conquerors."

Busy

Perhaps worse than distractions is the universal cancer of *busyness*. Someone sent me an email recently about *busyness* that is worth repeating:

> Satan called a worldwide convention. In his opening address to his evil angels, he said, "We can't keep the Christians from going to church. We can't keep them from reading their Bibles and knowing the truth. We can't even keep them from forming an intimate, abiding relationship experience in Christ. If they gain that connection with Jesus, our power over them is broken.
>
> So, let them go to their churches, let them have their conservative lifestyles, but steal their time, so they can't gain that relationship with Jesus Christ. This is what I want you to do, angels: distract them from gaining hold of their Savior and maintaining that vital connection throughout their day. "How shall we do this?" shouted

his angels. Keep them busy in the non-essentials of life and invent innumerable schemes to occupy their minds," he answered. "Tempt them to spend, spend, spend, and borrow, borrow, borrow. Persuade the wives to go to work for long hours and the husbands to work 6 or 7 days a week, 10-12 hours a day, so they can afford their empty lifestyles. Keep them from spending time with their children.

As their family fragments their home will offer no escape from the pressures of work! Over-stimulate their minds so that they cannot hear that still, small Voice. Entice them to play the radio or CD player whenever they drive and keep the TV, VCR, CDs and their PCs going constantly in their homes. See to it that every store and restaurant in the world plays non-biblical music constantly. This will jam their minds and break that union with Christ. Fill the coffee table with magazines and newspapers. Pound their minds with the news 24 hours a day. Invade their driving moments with billboards. Flood their mailboxes with junk mail, mail order catalogues, sweepstakes and every kind of newsletter and promotional offering, free products, services, and false hopes. Keep skinny, beautiful models on the magazines so the husbands will believe that external beauty is what's important, and they will become dissatisfied with their wives. HO! That will rapidly fragment those families!

Even in their recreation, let them be excessive. Have them return from their vacations exhausted, disquieted, and unprepared for the coming week. Don't let them go out in nature to reflect on God's wonders. Send them to amusement parks, sporting events, concerts and movies instead. Keep them busy, busy, and busy!! When they

Potholes on the Road to Discipleship

meet for spiritual fellowship, involve them in gossip and small talk so that they leave with troubled consciences and unsettled emotion. Go ahead, let them be involved in soul winning, but crowd their lives with so many good causes they have no time to seek power from Christ. Soon they will be working in their own strength, sacrificing their health and family for the good of the cause. It will work! It will work!"

The evil angels went eagerly to their assignments causing Christians everywhere to get busy, busy, busy, and to rush here, there, and everywhere.

-Author Unknown

Question: Has this been a successful strategy?

Stress

Joe is a young man we discipled. He had grown tremendously in the areas we are discussing, although he has been a believer for less than three years. He has learned how to soar. He knows how, by faith, to be controlled by the Spirit. Like all of us, he still has plenty of room for growth in his Christian life, but his basic direction in discipleship is good! He works hard, long hours at a famous computer company and is very good at what he does. He qualifies as–*any ole bush*.

One day he called and said, "I've had it. I'm stressed out." He said he was having trouble sleeping, had headaches, his stomach was bothering him, and he was unhappy with his job. Ever been there? Well, he knew that all those were symptoms of stress and anxiety and he knew also that God had provided a better way to handle things. We talked. I had just emailed some thoughts about that very issue to him. He had in fact, read it, but was not applying it to his present situation. "It helped to talk about it," he said.

ANY OLE BUSH

What do you do when you are stressed, exhausted, and worn down? Take a vacation, buy a new stereo, talk to a friend, go fishing? The Bible says that Jesus was tempted (stressed) in all points just as we are (Heb. 4:15). He knows what we are going through, and He cares. He is a living, loving Savior who wants us to come to Him and lean on Him when we are in trouble. Hebrews 4:15 in the New Living Translation says,

> *This High Priest of ours understands our weaknesses, for he faced all of the same testings we do, yet he did not sin. So let us come boldly to the throne of our gracious God. There we will receive his mercy, and we will find grace to help us when we need it most.*

Wonderful words! Is that where you go when you "have had it?"

Jesus knew what it was like to live in the real world. He grew up with the stigma of illegitimacy hanging over him. He lived in obscurity at near poverty levels for most of his life. He knew what it was to be physically weary, to be a *nobody*. He was an outcast among his peers; He was misunderstood, and falsely accused many times. His own family did not accept him. His closest friends deserted him. He was never married, lived alone, and owned nothing. He experienced a great deal of physical abuse and pain, was the victim of much social injustice, and ultimately was forsaken by God. He understands what it is like to have stress!

But today he invites us to come to him personally for grace, mercy, strength, and guidance. In Matthew 11:28-30 Jesus said,

> *"Come to me, all you who are weary and burdened, and I will give you rest. Take my yoke upon you and learn from me, for I am gentle and humble in heart, and you will find rest for your souls. For my yoke is easy and my burden is light."*

Potholes on the Road to Discipleship

Is this the truth? I believe it is and that is what brings tremendous peace and strength. So, why go anywhere else?

What is this yoke that God tells us is easy, and a perfect fit? Bruce Wilkinson, in a study of this verse, says that the yoke is the same yoke that Jesus wore, that is, to do the will of His Father. He said things like this repeatedly: "I do nothing to please myself; I honor my Father; I do not seek my own will; as I hear I speak; it is not my teaching, but my Father's; it is the Father living in me, doing His work."

"Not I but Christ." That is the secret of the Spirit-filled life. It means accepting the fact that I am dead to sin, but alive in Christ. It means denying self, and being obedient in everything, and allowing Him to be my life, bringing every thought captive to Him throughout the day. It includes being meek and humble like Jesus. The opposite of meek is self-assertive, and the opposite of humble is pride. That's why it is necessary to deny self and to come by faith to Jesus who is able to give us rest. We can be involved in many activities, doing many good things, and still miss the essential of denying self.

As I talked about all of this, with this young man from our church, Richard realized he had two choices or responses as to how to proceed. He could say, "Yeah, but…" and defend the valid reasons he had for feeling stressed and grumpy, or he could take a spiritual breath and confess his lack of trust in God's provision.

A *spiritual breath* is a term coined by Dr. Bill Bright. Just like physical breathing exhales the impurity (sin) of CO_2, and then inhales fresh oxygen (appropriates the Holy Spirit) he needed also to confess his own self centeredness, anger, stubbornness, unbelief and disobedience. Once he decided to do that, (it would only take a minute!) then he could again accept by faith the control of the indwelling, always present Holy Spirit and face the day expecting

Any Ole Bush

God to fill him with the peace, joy, and wisdom he needed. Marvelous! That is the way to "live!" And that is what is so exciting about discipling people; we can help them learn to walk in the Spirit!

A Nearly Disastrous Pothole–A Discipling Rescue

The Roosevelts had just left a church that had folded (after putting a lot of time and effort there) and started attending our Sunday school class. She was discouraged about her husband's spiritual state and hoped I would have a positive influence on him somehow.

She started telling Jan about the problems and inadequacies she saw in him. She complained about him not being a godly father, spending too much time at work and not having a quiet time. She nagged him about that repeatedly.

Jan suggested things like Titus 2:3-5, and used God's Word to point out what she needed. Easing off her husband's inadequacies might help too. This has resulted in an ongoing deepening friendship and almost a daily basis of sharing and encouragement over the phone for the past several years. The following is some of her story:

> On Valentine's Day in 1994, after almost 18 years of marriage, my husband asked me for a divorce. He was tired of living with an angry, critical wife. I realized that I was about to lose everything that really mattered to me. There was no one else that I wanted besides him. As I prayed that night, I realized the destructive nature of my sin. I realized that my husband's sins were between God and him. Because I had been focusing on his, I had not seen mine. I had been role-modeling this anger and bitterness to my children, undermining my husband's authority, and was tearing down my house with my own hands. God opened my eyes. That night I finally surrendered control of my life to Him (Feb. 14, 1994). All of a sudden, life became so simple! What a shabby counterfeit of victory I had accepted for so

Potholes on the Road to Discipleship

many years. I now had joy, peace, and comfort, yet none of my circumstances had changed. The next morning when my husband awoke, I told him what God had showed me, and asked his forgiveness. He said he forgave me, but he didn't really believe my story. It took my husband almost two years before he believed my heart had really changed.

Finally, he could deny it no longer. God convicted him that he needed to change his ways and his heart if he was going to be the spiritual leader in our home. As we both accepted the roles that God had for us, we found unspeakable peace and joy in our marriage. I needed to "walk in the spirit." I needed to continuously trust God. I took my discipler's advice and started reading great books. Two books in particular have been a tremendous help. *The Heart of the Problem* (workbook) by Drs. Henry Brandt and Kerry L. Skinner and *The Saving Life of Christ* by Major W. Ian Thomas. I have since then helped many different groups of women through this study guide with wonderful results. I have discovered that when I keep reading great books, I walk closer to Him because I am filling my mind with truth.

The most rewarding thing I have ever done is to disciple others. As I watched my mentor disciple others, I started noticing how she worked with God to take the problems in someone's life back to the Word of God. I have discipled women who are more mature than myself because I knew that God would give me all that this person needed because He was doing His work through me. He knew their hearts intimately and would see to all of their needs. It took all the pressure off of me to be wise or witty. What a joy it has been for me to watch Him work in the lives of others.

Any Ole Bush

Chapter Nine
Valuable Suggestions

I am sometimes asked to explain in some detail my Bible study and prayer habits. So, here goes:

Ever since I came to know Christ as Savior, I have wanted to know Christ better and live so He will be pleased with me. That is my lifelong motivation. I study the Bible with the intent of thinking like He thinks about everything. I study with the intent of getting to know Him more intimately and personally. It is a daily, ongoing renewal of my mind. Some days I may not feel like spending time in this way, so I have made it a point to simply do it anyway. I am always glad I do. My reading, studying, and pondering take many different forms.

High Tech Reading System

For several years I have used an extremely useful plan to help maintain a lifelong habit of reading through the Bible. I have read through the Bible several times in this fashion in the past few years. Instead of starting in Genesis and reading straight through, it is more interesting to read in different sections each day, but with a plan that will take you through the Bible over and over for the rest of your life. You can read each time as much (or as little) as you wish. I read for understanding and with the intent of obedience in every area to God.

I make a chart like the one below on a piece of scratch paper (or you can print one if you like) and keep it in my Bible. You can

ANY OLE BUSH

start anywhere you like. The example below starts with Genesis, Psalms, Proverbs, and Matthew, as shown. You read in Proverbs the chapter corresponding to the date. If it were January 4th, you would read Proverbs 4 that day. In the other books you read until you finish, then write in the name of the next book wherever you are in the chart, and continue on. When you fill up your chart, make another.

There is no pressure. Just read until God shows you something, and then stop and think, talk to the LORD about it, make some notes. Jot down each day where you stop and then start there the next time. I have used this system for more than fifteen years. It works well for me. Feel free to modify it anyway you like. Here is a sample chart, although this one is much neater than the ones I pencil on a piece of scratch paper: (a blank one is provided to copy in the appendix)

Book	Date Jan. 2	Date Jan. 5	Date	Date
Genesis	1			
Psalms	3	4		
Proverbs	2	5		
Matthew	1	2		

In the example above, I started on Jan 2 and read one chapter in Genesis, and thus would be ready to start in chapter 2 the next time I use this system. I also read 3 chapters in Psalms, and will start on chapter 4 next time. In Proverbs, I read the chapter for the day of the month (2), and in Matthew, I read one chapter, ready for chapter 2. I didn't read in this system for a couple of days, and then read just to chapter 4 in Psalms and read chapter 5 in Proverbs and one

Valuable Suggestions

chapter in Matthew. I read in Genesis that day. The next date(s) are blank, ready for your next visit. This system is simple and flexible.

I read until God reveals something to me personally, then I make some notes, mull over some principle, or maybe make a prolonged study of a topic. There is no pressure to read any certain amount, only until I know God is speaking to me. When God shows me some Truth in His Word, I have something to take with me for the day.

One time, my reading in this system took me to Matthew 22:37. I began thinking about this greatest of all commandments, which is to "Love the LORD your God with all your heart and with all your soul and with all your mind." How could I possibly do that? Over the next two months I spent a considerable amount of time looking up, studying, and pondering all the verses I could find having to do with God's love for me. It has been one of the most valuable and life-changing studies of my life. It caused me to develop an unshakeable conviction that God really does love me personally. It has flavored my worldview, my Bible reading, my attitudes, and the way I treat people. Valuable stuff! And it came out of my high-tech reading system!

Topics and Verses

I also enjoy studying topics, such as marriage, money, faith, the Holy Spirit, grace, and a host of others. I make notes as I study and keep the notes in three-ring binders with a computerized, up-to-date list so I can (usually) find things. This has been incredibly useful in preparation for teaching and helping others.

One beautiful afternoon on a mountain in California, I took a clipboard, sat down under a big tree, and spent about three hours mentally digging (meditating) into Matthew 4:19. "Come, follow me," Jesus said, "and I will make you fishers of men." I simply wrote the verse vertically down the left margin of my paper, and then concentrated my thoughts on each word, writing down as much as I could about each word (like chewing a cud.) I didn't worry about format, but just wrote whatever occurred to me. I took plenty of time. I asked myself questions and prayed for God to reveal what He wanted me to know. I didn't have to hurry. That study has stayed fresh in my mind for more than forty-five years! Anyone can do that! Why don't you try it yourself on one of your favorite verses.

Here is what I had on my pad when I came down the mountain:

Follow

That means I need to look at the one I follow. Abide. Walk. There is an invitation here, an option. Keep within sight. Requires a leader. Submission to the leader. Can't have my own way. Available to every believer. Requires movement. Jesus said this some fifteen times. 1 Kings 18:21 says, "If the Lord is God, follow him." (I couldn't think of anything else here, so, I went on to the next word.)

Me

Not angels, not teachings or rules, or even His example, but "Me." "I will personally lead you." Who said that? The King of Kings, Lord of Lords. The loving, powerful, patient, omniscient, omnipotent, Sovereign God! With Him there are no emergencies, no mistakes, no tragedies. He knows all my sins and capacities, past and future. He is alive. Only He can provide forgiveness, peace, power, and purpose. Colossians 1 and John 1 speak of Him. What a leader! I can follow Him without doubt, or fear, or question. Almighty God!!

And I Will

Not *might* or *could*. A flat, ungarnished, bald, simple, naked statement...no disclaimers or loopholes. "I WILL." Who said that? Jesus, the Lord. The Lord Jesus Christ will. That kills the "*BUT* what about..." that I think of almost at once.

Valuable Suggestions

Make

Refashion, shape, change, cut down. Make me what I am *NOT* at this point. I am inadequate. It may be painful, this *making*. What changes are needed here? Love, boldness, filling, motivation, transformed mind, humility, and obedience are a few needs that come to mind. It is more than a bunch of qualities. The extent of my need is huge: *natural* to *supernatural*. Not just experience. Not education or increase in ability or discipline. From the old man to the new man. Dying to self. Only Jesus can *make* me what I need to be.

You

Who me? Yes you! Whoever you are. Who am I? I know now that my old sin nature is dead. I died with Christ. That old selfish nature that was dead spiritually, with no power, rebellious, helpless, sinful, and separated from God–is gone according to the Bible. My new nature is alive to God. I am a Son of God, Heir of God, a saint, loved by God, clothed with the righteousness of Christ, accepted, adopted, seated, and accepted. A new person. That is the real me. It is what God says I am–in Christ! Wow! That is the *me* that He will make a fisher of men.

Fishers

Spoken to fishermen who knew what fishing meant. Jesus knew how to talk to people. Fishing was hard, continuous, and time consuming work. Not fly casting on vacations just for the fun of it. And catching is the fun, not just fishing. Fishermen spend lots of time preparing to fish. There are many ways: nets, lines, dynamite, or a sign on the boat *Fish Jump in Here*. Use what works. Go where the fish are. Need to be there when the fish are there! Then, don't sit in the boat and discuss how to catch fish–put the lines in the water!

Any Ole Bush

Of Men

All men. On all frontiers of unbelief. Everywhere. All kinds. All around me. They are without purpose, without life. Lost. Jesus loves them all. I don't, but He does! He is not willing that any should perish.

SO, Jesus says here to:
- Fish for men–nope
- Catch fish–nope
- Develop a program for fish catching–wrong again

He said:
- "FOLLOW ME." That is my part.
- "I will make you fishers of men." That is His part.

Therefore, it seems to me that if I follow Him, fishing for men will happen!

> If we are not fishing—WE ARE NOT FOLLOWING HIM

Reading Great Books

Reading books is a way of tapping the resources of great men of God both of the past and the present. I try not to read good books, since that would take away the time I need for the great ones. Very few of us have enough time to read both! "What are the great books," you ask? That will depend on whom you ask, of course. If you were to ask me, I would refer you to a list included in this book. When I first realized the importance of reading great books, I was blessed to have someone give me a copy of Wilbur Smith's book *Profitable Bible Study*. He was a genius in the field of Christian books, so I decided to listen to his advice. This book was copyrighted in 1939 and published in 1953! A friend gave it to me in 1962 and I devoured it. One of the chapters is called, "The First One

Valuable Suggestions

Hundred Books for the Bible Student's Library." I started looking for those books, and have added a few of my own over the years. It was a wonderful start for me.

A quote from Wilbur Smith's book that is worth saving:

> *Not merely worthless literature should be sacrificed, but, for the sake of the best, we must sacrifice much which would be very valuable to use if we had not the best. We must sacrifice a great many good books; otherwise we shall be very large readers of comparatively small thought.*[1]

Exactly! His quote about meditation is equally important.

> *The intellect gathers and prepares the food upon which we are to feed. In meditation the heart takes it in and feeds on it.*[2]

I always keep great books on my desk, and take one with me whenever I go anywhere (such as a doctor's office) just in case some reading time comes available. It always does! It is my firm conviction that a godly person must be a voracious reader. Lots of folks (especially men) tell me they don't like to read. "Pity!"–say I. "Read anyway!"

I also find it profitable to study how God shaped the people of the Bible. Many valuable books have been written about Bible characters such as David, Abraham, Paul, Rahab, Jezebel, Moses, Peter, John, and many others. Great insights can be gained for your own personal character development as you read how God molded each person He used.

I also talk to God (pray) about what He is telling me through the Scripture and these great books. I choose a quiet place where I can be alone so that my time of prayer is uninterrupted. "By Himself, alone" is a phrase frequently used in reference to Jesus spending time with His Heavenly Father.

ANY OLE BUSH

These aspects of study contribute to my own personal spiritual understanding and growth–*IN CHRIST*. Every day, preparation is necessary for scheduled meetings with disciples, Sunday school lessons, and writing my weekly email.

Good Stuff, my weekly email, is simply a reflection on whatever has been on my spiritual front burner lately. It is gratifying to see how often God guides me into some subject, verse, or principle that someone needed that week! I often receive wonderful comments of how these help others. Many of the recipients are forwarding these short observations to their friends and relatives as well. My website (www.bertsgoodstuff.com) contains all of these weekly items where people can easily download and print them.

How do I manage to get enough time to do all this? Glad you asked. I have a conviction that every person has all the time we need to do everything that God intends for us to do–if we don't waste that time with other good or bad things. Would you buy that? When I was a practicing anesthesiologist, there were many times I worked very long hours. Discretionary time was valuable and scarce, so I made my time with God a high priority. That took the form of resisting all sorts of usual things that soak up time, such as medical committee meetings, social events, TV (the biggest of all time-gobblers), sports, (windsurfing is probably the only biblical exception here…?) travel, hobbies, magazines, newspapers, concerts, movies, and games. Not that any of those are bad, but I just wanted to avoid having those things steal the time I wanted to spend with God and my family.

Now that I am retired, there is of course, much more time available. Many men tell themselves they have to work now, and will spend time with God when there is "a more convenient" time. I believe that is a huge mistake. A father is vitally important to the kids when they are young. That is when they most need a godly

Valuable Suggestions

father who takes the time to be with God daily and to meet the multiple needs of his family. My kids have their own families now. Any time not spent with them in their vital growing years is gone. I am more grateful than words can express for the choices I made about those issues back then. I have been hugely blessed.

What About Prayer?

Sometimes I wonder just how deeply I believe in prayer, since I have more time to pray than I use for that purpose! On the other hand, I do pray often, not so much at special times, but as I go through the day and as needs surface. I pray (not just read) during my time of Bible study. A prayer notebook is a helpful tool to use during those times you set aside for several hours of meditation and prayer. The notebook I use has many articles and helps about prayer, praise, confession, repentance, and worship. Also, I have a detailed list of needs and prayer requests for people I know.

These memorized Bible passages are very special to me in regard to prayer. I would certainly like for others to pray for me as described in these passages. You might want to use them for your own use.

> *And this I pray: that your love may abound yet more and more and extend to its fullest development in knowledge and all keen insight [that your love may display itself in greater depth of acquaintance and more comprehensive discernment],*
>
> *So that you may surely learn to sense what is vital, and approve and prize what is excellent and of real value [recognizing the highest and the best, and distinguishing the moral differences], and that you may be untainted and pure and unerring and blameless [so that with hearts sincere and certain and unsullied, you may approach] the day of Christ [not stumbling nor causing others to stumble].*
>
> **Philippians 1:9-10, AMP**

Any Ole Bush

For this reason also, since the day we heard of it, we have not ceased to pray for you and to ask that you may be filled with the knowledge of His will in all spiritual wisdom and understanding, so that you will walk in a manner worthy of the Lord, to please Him in all respects, bearing fruit in every good work and increasing in the knowledge of God; strengthened with all power, according to His glorious might, for the attaining of all steadfastness and patience; joyously giving thanks to the Father, who has qualified us to share in the inheritance of the saints in Light.

Colossians 1:9-12, NAS

All of this and more I seek to "commit to faithful men" as 2 Timothy 2:2 says. I want to help others to love God, to develop strong yearning to know Him, to please Him, and to walk under the influence of the Holy Spirit. Scripture and prayer is the way to accomplish that spiritual growth. I prepare for meeting with people by thus filling my *vat* with truth and love for God, and then trust Him to use what is in there! I trust Him to guide my mind in preparing what I may say to them. God knows what the people need and He knows how to use my preparation to help them most. I don't depend on my wisdom, but on His. I only vibrate their tympanic membrane (ear drum)–God has to change their heart. It is not what I do, it is what He does through me. That is why the most valuable thing I can do for a disciple is to abide in Christ, and saturate my mind with His Word, and pray. And that is why *any ole bush* will do!

What to Look For

It is easy to become complacent, and think "I have it made now," and drift away from absolute and total daily dependence on God. One day, with my mind full of these great principles and truths, I drove my 1985 Jeep to get the mandatory emissions test. It had previously had trouble passing the test, requiring some tweaking by mechanics.

Valuable Suggestions

I had to wait in a long line for the test, and began to think: "I bet it won't pass this time, and then I will have to take it to the mechanic again and waste a bunch of time getting it ready for another test, and it will be expensive and inconvenient, bla bla bla etc., etc." I was trying to read some stuff for a Bible study I was to lead that night. The line was moving slow. I was getting more disgruntled by the minute. Then I thought, "Wait a minute! What have you been teaching people about stuff like this? To pray and trust God with it all," I answered myself. "Your peace and contentment does not depend on this Jeep!" So, I stopped grumbling and muttering and turned to the Lord and said, Lord I trust you with this little problem. If it passes–fine. If it doesn't pass–no problem. You will give me wisdom and whatever else I need to get it fixed. I actually stopped grumbling, relaxed, and enjoyed the rest of the day! (It passed!)

This is a small example of what it means to know, but not own the truth. I have had many such opportunities, and so have you. On a much bigger scale, that is exactly the way Paul handled all of his problems and trials. The principles are the same. Secondary, controversial issues tend to cause division, confusion, and spawn fruitless discussion. We try to avoid them. Some people like to endlessly discuss these things because, in my opinion, it does not commit them to anything.

Pride in the heart of the one who is doing the discipling is a big danger and all of us are very prone to it. The opposite of pride is humility. Andrew Murray defines humility as "the place of entire dependence upon God."[3] I need awareness of that every single day!

Another trap is to believe that a little growth is evidence of a huge and real commitment to God. Often, we are unaware of huge defects and sins lying just below the surface. Sometimes, we justify these sins by focusing on the little growth in our lives. The Bible says that we "deceive ourselves" and we also deceive each other; many times deliberately.

Any Ole Bush

It takes time for people to grow spiritually. Allow for it. On the other hand, "don't hold hands with the half-hearted."

After Finishing the 1-ON-1

Often we study through a book called *The Heart of The Problem*, by Drs. Henry Brandt and Kerry L. Skinner. We plan to study one unit every two weeks. We discuss many real situations covered there. It is saturated with Bible verses applied to the problems all of us face. Or, we may study a book in the Bible, or a topic. At other times we will study one of the assigned books that we were not able to cover while going through the 1-ON-1. It depends on what we perceive is needed most at the time. We are firm believers in reading great books, not good books, but great ones. Read only the best, and read them more than once.

We have had many people tell us that great books have been incredibly helpful in their quest to be transformed.

Bottom Line Stuff

"I no longer live, but Christ lives in me." (Gal. 2:20)
- I can't, but He can.
- Keep the main thing, the main thing!
- The Holy Spirit lives within every believer. We are jars of clay, containing deity.
- Jesus said to be filled/controlled by the Holy Spirit, continuously.
- Jesus said to make disciples.
- His part is to live His life in us; our part is to be willing; i.e. to live by faith, plus, to be obedient in everything.
- Therefore, anyone can do it; *any ole bush will do.*
- Life is short, don't waste (any of) it.
- Do you need to change anything?
- Now is the only day you really have.

Valuable Suggestions

And the things you have heard me say in the presence of many witnesses entrust to reliable men who will also be qualified to teach others.

2 Timothy 2:2

Don't forget the appendix for a list of great books to read!

Now What?

Ask God to use you in the life of some of your business associates, friends, or family–perhaps your own kids. If you are equipped, and willing, your phone will ring! Ask people if they would like to study with you in this manner. Be available. Expect God to use you.

---

[1] Wilbur Smith, *Profitable Bible Study*, (Boston, Massachusetts, W.A. Wilde Company, 1953), 205.
[2] Ibid, 63. (Some of these books can be found at www.bookfinder.com or www.amazon.com)
[3] Andrew Murray, *Humility: The Journey Toward Holiness*, (Minneapolis, Minnesota, Christian Literature Crusade, 2001), 16.

Any Ole Bush

Appendix
Great Books to Read

Title	Author
The Amplified New Testament	(Use as study Bible)
The Saving Life Of Christ	Major W. Ian Thomas
The Heart Of The Problem (workbook)	Henry Brandt and Kerry L. Skinner
Marriage God's Way	Henry Brandt and Kerry L. Skinner
The Word For The Wise	Henry Brandt and Kerry L. Skinner
Victory In Christ	Charles Trumbull
Grace Walk	Steve McVey
Grace Rules	Steve McVey
The Knowledge Of The Holy	A.W. Tozer
The Spiritual Life	Andrew Murray
Humility	Andrew Murray
The True Vine	Andrew Murray
Like Christ	Andrew Murray
The God You Can Know	Dan DeHaan
The Normal Christian Life	Watchman Nee
Sit, Walk, Stand	Watchman Nee
Knowing God	J.I. Packer
The Greatest Thing In The World	Henry Drummond
Fresh Wind Fresh Fire	Jim Cymbala
The Lost Art Of Disciplemaking	LeRoy Eims
Intimacy With The Almighty	Charles R. Swindoll
Believer's Bible Commentary	Wm. MacDonald
The Master Plan Of Evangelism	Robert Coleman
Personal Disciple Making (1996)	Christopher Adsit
Share Jesus Without Fear	William Fay
Margin	Richard A. Swenson
Half Time	Bob Buford
To Train Up A Child	Michael and Debi Pearl
Shepherding A Child's Heart	Ted Tripp
Tender Warrior	Stu Weber

Any Ole Bush

Title	Author
Finishing Strong	Steve Farrar
The Mark Of A Man	Elisabeth Elliot
Evidence That Demands A Verdict	Josh McDowell
Reflecting His Image	K.P. Yohannan
Heaven	Jonathan Edwards
Love Life for Every Married Couple	Dr. Ed Wheat
Don't Waste Your Life	John Piper
The Rest Of The Gospel	Dan Stone

Primarily for the Ladies

Title	Author
Creative Counterpart	Linda Dillow
Intended for Pleasure	Dr. Ed Wheat
You Can Be the Wife of a Happy Husband	Darien Cooper

Book	Date	Date	Date	Date	Date	Date	Date	Date	Date